CAREERS
IN HIGH TECH

CAREERS
IN HIGH TECH

NICK BASTA

97-1895

VGM Career Horizons
a division of *NTC Publishing Group*
Lincolnwood, Illinois USA

Library of Congress Cataloging-in-Publication Data

Basta, Nicholas, 1954–
    Careers in high tech / Nicholas Basta.

            p.   cm. — (VGM professional careers series)
        ISBN 0-8442-4180-6   (hardcover)   :   ISBN 0-8442-4181-4
    (softcover)
        1. Engineers—Vocational guidance.   2. Scientists—Vocational
          guidance.
        3. Technologists—Vocational guidance.   I. Title.
        II. Series.
    TA157.B3418   1992
    620′.0023—dc20   91-42919
                                                                                     CIP

1993 Printing

Published by VGM Career Horizons, a division of NTC Publishing Group.
© 1992 by NTC Publishing Group, 4255 West Touhy Avenue,
Lincolnwood (Chicago), Illinois 60646-1975 U.S.A.

  3 4 5 6 7 8 9 0 VP 9 8 7 6 5 4 3 2

CONTENTS

ABOUT THE AUTHOR

Nicholas Basta has worked as a business and technology journalist in New York for over ten years, focusing on manufacturing, government policies, environmental activities, computer technology, and professional careers. He has been a regular contributor to *Chemical Engineering, Graduating Engineer, Career World,* the Wall Street Journal's *National Business Employment Weekly, Business Week Careers,* and *High Technology.* He is the author of *Opportunities in Engineering Careers,* published by NTC Publishing Group, and *Top Professions,* published by Peterson's Guides.

Basta graduated in 1977 from Princeton University with a B.S. degree in chemical engineering.

Part One
Introduction to
High Tech

THE NATURE OF HIGH TECH

They are companies with odd names, usually with X's, *-tech*, *-tex*, or *-gen* in their label. They have futuristic-looking headquarters buildings, often designed and constructed by the company executives and often located in remote, scenic parts of North America, such as New Hampshire, Oregon, or British Columbia. Their executives may drive Ferraris or Jaguars into the company parking lot—or may commute via bicycle. Usually, these executives have a hard time describing to outsiders what the company does.

Who are these companies? Because of the varieties of businesses they are in, ranging from medicine to energy to electronics, they are hard to unify under one umbrella. Wall Street analysts, wanting to make life simple by doing just that, have called them "high technology" or "high tech" companies. They are revolutionizing industry, and their products are changing our lives.

For well over a decade, high tech companies have garnered the spotlight in business circles. There is something exciting about turning new scientific discoveries directly into products that make our lives more comfortable or that provide strength to manufacturing and commerce. The list of companies is long, and growing longer each year. In computers, there are companies such as Compaq, Microsoft, DEC, Convex, and Autodesk. In pharmaceuticals, there are companies such as Genentech, Amgen, or Biogen. In energy, there are Solarex and American Ref-Fuel. In electronics, there are companies such as Intel, Motorola, Tectronix, Texas Instruments, and others.

Standing behind these smaller firms (some of which have grown to billion-dollar size over the past ten years) are some mighty industrial giants that were themselves the entrepreneurially driven high tech firms of previous generations. These include Xerox, International Business Machines (IBM), Hewlett-Packard, Exxon, Merck, Dow Chemical, Du Pont, Boeing, and General Motors.

The small, entrepreneurial companies that are the source of many technological innovations are the heart of high tech. But there is often as much (or more) high technology required to *use* high technology as there is to develop it. A good example might be a designer who works at what is called an engineering workstation. These workstations are high-powered microcomputers equipped with highly sophisticated software (programs). The designer might be doing something as "low tech" as creating a new shoe design or writing new specifications for a bolt. Nevertheless, a knowledge of computers and engineering is essential to this design work, and that designer can truly call himself or herself a high tech worker.

Think of this book as a ticket to a rollercoaster ride through high technology. The sights and sounds are dazzling and a little scary. High technology can certainly be intimidating to think about as a place in which to find a career. But relatively few people set up their entire careers that way. Most of them, having discovered that they are fairly good at math or science as students, decide to study science or engineering in college. Once they graduate, they find people and companies working in exciting new fields, and they want to participate themselves. A job is obtained, and the new graduate begins pitching in with contributions on how a technology should be developed or applied. That worker can then go in many different directions—teaching the use of the new technology to customers or to students; selling the technology to buyers; helping manufacture a product; helping install or service the product; or writing about it so that users know how it works. If the worker is successful in these endeavors, he or she may rise in the management of the company, becoming an administrator who may not ever write computer code or touch a laboratory beaker, but who guides the efforts of other high tech workers.

Thus, to remain in high tech it is not essential to be the world's sharpest scientist in some area of technology. What is most essential, in fact, is to be eternally curious about how things work (or should work) and to be willing to learn continuously. Some high tech researchers stop working after five or so years and go back to school to learn a new area of science or technology. All of them must seek to reeducate themselves on a regular basis to keep up with the advances in their fields of technology.

It is this curiosity and willingness to learn that distinguishes the high tech worker from most others. In many other professions, you learn a skill in college or immediately after graduation and spend the rest of your career refining that skill and gaining experience in using it. That's not bad, and many people enjoy the chance to do one thing especially well. But that's not the outlook of the high tech worker. "You shouldn't just keep getting to be better and better" at one type of work, a career counselor was recently quoted as saying in *Business Week*. "You need a diversity of skills in your career portfolio. The more you have, the more marketable you are."

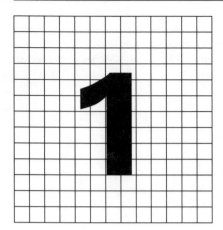

SCIENCE AND TECHNOLOGY

WHAT EXACTLY IS TECHNOLOGY?

It might seem logical to have answered this question right off. However, it is appropriate to raise the point here, where the great division between science on the one hand and engineering or industrial technology on the other hand becomes apparent.

Science is something that you probably have become familiar with during various high school courses. Science is the body of knowledge that addresses what the physical universe is made of and how it functions. In the history of science dating back over 3,000 years, science and philosophy (the study of all types of knowledge) were intertwined. Ancient Greek philosophers, for example, attempted to explain the motions of the planets or the varieties of living things strictly through mental exercises. Conversely, they reasoned through moral and religious issues by looking at the natural world around them.

Starting around 1600, and becoming widespread in Europe during the 1700s, a new concept of science arose. Science became the practice of proving the unknown through experimentation. If you could conduct an experiment to prove the presence of, say, metal in soil, then you would make a contribution to the body of scientific knowledge. If you could not conceive of an experiment that would answer such a question, then the question was not one that could properly be addressed by science. (There are thousands of such questions that are not properly addressed by science; these are the proper sphere of religion, morality, and philosophy.)

Usually, science addresses fundamental questions about the universe, such as how matter and energy combine, or what the fundamental particles of material things are. By studying such things, scientists hope to gain a better understanding of the universe. Once this understanding has been achieved, it can be applied to improve human conditions—and this is where technology comes in. Technologists take the new knowledge that scientists have uncovered and seek to apply it in ways that are useful to humanity.

Technology surrounds us from the moment we wake up until we fall asleep. Technology has made possible the comfortable lifestyles that many of us enjoy. It has also created many of the ills our society faces today, from such environmental catastrophes as the depletion of the ozone layer to the harmful effects of television on the education of the young. Some people believe that technology is the culmination of 4,000 years of human advancement, enabling us to travel to the stars or live under the oceans. Others believe that technology is an inhuman force, pushing humanity in directions that it would not go if left to itself.

Technology is neither as great a force as some believe nor as beneficial as some of its proponents claim. Resolving questions about the usefulness of technology has involved many thinkers in recent years.

One of the best analyses of technology came from Samuel Florman, a civil engineer in the New York area who wrote a classic book, *The Existential Pleasures of Engineering,* in 1976 (St. Martin's Press). In it, Florman argues that technology cannot be the unstoppable force that some people think simply because it so often fails. Every year, thousands of new products are offered to the consumer; the majority of these fail to sell well within that year. Those failures imply that the everyday consumer still can choose among a variety of options, and the technological option is only one of them. While there are new types of technology continually being offered to the public, only those that meet a desired end succeed commercially. Technological success often does not translate into commercial success.

Conversely, there have been many technologies that have changed our lives immeasurably. The telephone, electricity, and the railroad were the technological marvels of the nineteenth century; the automobile, the television, and the personal computer have revolutionized twentieth-century life.

WHO WORKS IN TECHNOLOGY?

While it takes individual consumers to make a technology succeed, it takes inventors and innovators to dream up the technology to begin with. The choices you make in what subjects to study and what industries to join will shape the future course of technology. Here, the personal issue of science versus technology comes to the fore. Most professional scientists (which is to say, those with a doctoral degree) are engaged in research and development (R&D). Many of them work on college campuses; others work in private firms or for large corporations, but frequently in the R&D lab.

The workday of such professional scientists is not too far from the experiences you may have had in high school science laboratories. The experiment is the crucial learning mechanism. R&D scientists run experiments, analyze the results, and share those results with other scientists to arrive at theories of why the experiments came out the way they did.

Engineers and industrial technology graduates typically do not work in laboratories. They work at factories, in design offices, or in the field, taking measurements of, say, the chemical purity of underground water and then seeking useful applications of those measurements. In this specific case, the goal may be to find a new source of drinkable water or to track pollutants moving through the ground. Then they will check the textbooks or studies that scientists have written to determine what the proper course of action will be. Often, technologically oriented workers must make decisions in the absence of necessary scientific knowledge. This isn't as difficult as it sounds—engineers can conduct their own experiments to find out how something will work, and then use that knowledge to design a bridge or build an aircraft, all without the fundamental understanding that science provides.

In fact, it is quite frequently the case that some knotty technological problem eventually leads to new scientific knowledge. Scientists hear about a problem from engineers or other technologically oriented workers, and then try to reason through the fundamental facts that would explain or answer the problem. One example of this is the flurry of research going on today in materials research on "warm" superconductors. Scientists at IBM's laboratories in Zurich, Switzerland, working with researchers at various U.S. universities, first developed the new materials. When engineers tried to build wires or other large objects from the material, however, they discovered that when they attempted to mold or form the object, the superconducting properties were lost. These results were passed back to the scientists, who will use them to gain a better understanding of how superconductivity operates, regardless of the materials involved.

There are, of course, scientists who work primarily outside the laboratory—even on the factory floor—and engineers who work exclusively in laboratories. Generally speaking, any engineer or scientist with a doctoral degree (Ph.D.) is a candidate for laboratory research. Scientists and engineers with master's or bachelor's degrees perform various functions in a variety of settings:

1. At manufacturers, these high tech workers are involved in production, design, quality control, testing, and management

2. At consulting firms (which typically have manufacturing clients), they work as designers and specifiers. The most common form of consulting is construction services: for example, designing and then building a skyscraper or highway.

3. In the services sector of the economy, such as banking, communications, or transportation, engineers and scientists provide specialized advice and consultation. For a bank, to take one example, electrical engineers and computer scientists may work to design and install a combined computing/communications network.

4. In government, engineers and scientists provide a diverse array of services. Some work as researchers in the network of national laboratories, performing experiments just as a researcher at a private company or a university would. Others act as administrators or program directors, guiding the efforts of other scientists. Still others are involved in the regulation of commerce, for example establishing standards for communications, foods and drugs, environmental performance, and health and safety.

HOW MANY PEOPLE WORK IN HIGH TECH FIELDS?

All high tech workers deal with numbers—so let's look at some numbers that sum up this information. For U.S. data, the Bureau of Labor Statistics (BLS) provides detailed assessments of the numbers of workers with various types of occupations in *Occupational Projections and Training Data* (1990). The listing is comprehensive, covering 250 occupations ranging from government chief executives to parking lot attendants, from nuclear engineers to dancers. Table 1 provides a count of the professions most closely related to high tech work. BLS also uses economic projections to make an estimate of future job growth in these occupations (columns 3 and 4). Column 5 shows the single largest employer of each profession, which usually represents about 20–40 percent of the job positions. Most of the professions are broadly distributed throughout all sectors of U.S. manufacturing.

It is extremely important to note that, while the average growth over the current decade from all occupations that BLS studied is just over 15 percent, all but three of the twenty-two high tech occupations listed in Table 1 have projected growth rates above that. In the case of computer workers and electrical engineers, the rate of growth is nearly three times that of the general workforce.

The equivalent data on Canada is not available. However, the Canadian Council of Professional Engineers recently made a detailed assessment of current and future prospects in engineering. The results are shown in Table 2.

These are only some of the engineers at work in Canada today; the study estimates that there were about 89,000 engineers at work in Canada in 1990; in terms of the supply of new engineering graduates joining the workforce during the 1990s, the Council projects that this number will increase to about 127,000 by 2000. However, demand will be sub-

Table 1 Occupational projection, 1990–2005

	1990*	2005*	% change	primary employer
*employment, 1,000's				
computer systems analyst	463	829	79	data processing services
operations and systems researcher	57	100	73	data processing services
medical scientist	19	31	66	hospitals
computer programmer	565	882	56	data processing services
electrical/electronic engineer	426	571	34	communication equipment
electrical and electronic technologist	363	488	34	machinery & equipment
engineering or science manager	315	423	34	eng'g & architect. services
biological scientist	62	83	34	federal gov't
physician	580	776	34	physicians' offices
civil engineer	198	257	30	eng'g & architect. services
agricultural and food scientist	25	32	27	federal gov't
clinical laboratory technologist	258	321	24	hospitals
science and mathematics technician	246	305	24	education
mechanical engineer	233	289	22	eng'g & architect. services
geologist, oceanographer	48	58	22	petroleum, natural gas
metallurgist and material engineer	18	22	21	aircraft & parts
TOTAL, ALL OCCUPATIONS IN BLS	122573	147191	20	
aeronautical/astronautical engineer	73	88	20	aircraft & parts
industrial engineer	135	160	19	communications, aircraft
chemist	83	96	16	drugs
computer and peripheral equipment operator	320	361	13	banks & financial services
chemical engineer	48	54	12	chemicals, plastics
mathematical scientist	22	24	9	federal & state gov't
physicist and astronomer	20	21	5	business services

Source: selected data from BLS

stantially higher—around 170,000. Overall engineering demand growth will be on the order of 45 percent, according to the study, which is dramatically above the norm for the total Canadian workforce.

Further insight into the Canadian employment situation comes from the Canadian Labour Market and Productivity Centre, which unveiled a

Table 2 Canadian engineering projections

Engineering speciality	1990 employment	2000 (projected) employment	% change
Chemical	6065	8600	42
Civil	28793	40938	42
Electrical	30869	44406	44
Mechanical	23281	33695	45

Source: Dalcor Innoventures Ltd., *Engineering the Future.* (Commissioned by the Canadian Engineering Manpower Board, 1990)

study in *Indicator* (the official publication of the Canadian Engineering Manpower Board) in 1990 called "The High-Tech Sector: A Growing Source of Jobs." The Centre conducted a telephone survey of various companies that belong to its definition of high tech industries. The survey found that some 350,000 workers were employed in high tech industries, and that job growth was rising at nearly four times the rate of all types of Canadian jobs (the projected rate of increase was 3.8 percent per year in 1990 and 1991 versus 1 percent for the nation as a whole). Most of the firms in this group reported that they were experiencing difficulties in filling job openings. The most difficult to fill were in the "professional, scientific, and technical" category, where 59 percent of those interviewed had "significant" or "some" difficulty in filling openings.

SUMMARY

To recap, the first thing to remember about high tech industries is that they represent many different types of manufacturing and services—they are not just manufacturers of computers and electronics.

The second point to recall is that the core of the high tech workforce is engineers and scientists engaged in research and development. The sciences include all the physical sciences (chemistry, physics, and so on) and biological sciences. All the engineering disciplines are included, as well as a variety of programs called engineering or industrial technology. There is also an important place among high tech companies for liberal arts graduates, in such positions as communications, patent law, or business administration.

The third point is that these workers are engaged in *technological* development and not normally pure scientific research. Because, very often, such research leads directly to commercially useful concepts, the overlap between scientific research and technology is large.

The fourth point is that most of the scientific and engineering disciplines that compose the high-tech workforce are projected to have growth rates over this decade that are considerably higher than the growth rate for the total workforce. This is true both in the United States and in Canada.

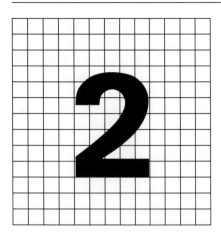

WHAT IS HIGH TECHNOLOGY?

If you ask five people what high technology is, you are likely to get five different answers. Those differences point to a key element about high tech careers: they are what people make them.

Most people think of high technology as something to do with computers and electronics. Those two industries are very much part of the high tech landscape, but after those two, there is very little consensus over what else is high tech. Biotechnology—the manipulation of genetic material to develop new drugs or diagnostic techniques—is often mentioned, but biotechnology is only a part of the pharmaceutical industry, so let's include pharmaceuticals as well. Lasers—a special type of light that is strong enough to cut through metal—are also often thought of as high tech, but the largest use of lasers today is in telecommunications, which includes the telephone, satellites, radio, television, cable TV, and so forth. Those industries should be added to the list, too.

You may have heard recently about warm superconductivity—the invention of metals that can carry an electrical current with no energy loss. The phenomenon of superconductivity has been understood for most of this century, but to achieve it, special alloys had to be chilled to near absolute zero (–460°F). In the past six years, new superconducting metals have been devised that still need to be chilled, but only to around –283°F—still very cold, but much easier to achieve. To be useful, these new materials need to be formed into sheets or wires, and this calls in the knowledge of the metalworking industries. Are they another high tech candidate?

Looking in another direction—that of living things—we find that medical doctors are employing a host of new devices. These include CAT scans, magnetic resonance imaging (MRI), polymerase chain reactions (PCR), and many other diagnostic tools. (All of these technologies will be explained in more detail later in this book.) Most of these are recent developments in medical research and involved the skills of dozens of scientists to create. So, shall we include medicine as another high tech industry?

Though this listing could go on and on, there are at least three elements common to all these industries and inventions:

1. They are all innovations based on scientific and engineering research.
2. They represent a radically *new* way of doing things—they're not simply an improvement or modification of existing techniques.
3. They are *commercial,* which simply means that companies are in business today using them for products that are bought and sold.

Let's examine the significance of each of these points.

THE CHARACTERISTICS OF HIGH TECH INDUSTRIES

First, that high technology is the fruit of "scientific and engineering research" simply means that scientists and engineers were the inventors or developers of the innovations. In the business world, there are thousands of new products or ways of doing things that are invented each year. A bank, for example, might innovate by offering a new savings plan for depositors. A restaurant might innovate by devising a new type of cuisine. These developments are indeed new, but they are not technical in nature. (They may, however, be as profitable to the company offering them as any high tech product.) So, obviously, high technology involves the use of technology.

Second, high technology is radically new. Many companies employ scientists, engineers, and other professionals to make improvements or modifications to existing products. A chemical company, for example, might find a way to make a plastic without wasting any of the raw materials. An aerospace manufacturer might improve the fuel efficiency of its aircraft by adapting engine modifications. These developments are technical in nature, but they are only an extension of existing practices. However, when a computer company performs research on a parallel processing supercomputer (again, this term will be explained later), that represents something very new to the field. That makes it high technology.

The third point, that the innovation is commercial, is what distinguishes "pure" from "applied" scientific research. These two terms have traditionally indicated the separation between scientific research that is performed for its own sake, as a way of increasing the knowledge of humanity, and that which is done in order to make money. Examples of pure scientific research can be found in astronomy—where scientists study how the stars evolve or whether there are other planets in the galaxy. Another example is in mathematics, where scientists examine logical ways to manipulate numbers and other symbols, usually simply for the joy of being able to do so.

The funny thing about most types of pure research is that over time, discoveries that "pure" scientists make become something very useful to the "applied" scientists who are looking to solve everyday problems. To cite just one example, scientists in the 1930s and 1940s developed particle accelerators—machines that could speed up atomic particles and ram them into each other—as a way to study atomic physics. By the 1970s and 1980s, these types of machines were being used to build microelectronic components; now they are being talked about as a way to cure cancer. Neither of these results was remotely thought of when scientists first devised the accelerators. They simply wanted to look more deeply into the atom. But the knowledge gained by those original scientists was found to be incredibly useful to later generations of researchers.

It used to be true that there was a sharp distinction between pure and applied research and that all applied research was built on what pure scientists had done before. That distinction—never universally true to begin with—is fading from today's scene. Many types of applied research uncover some intriguing new property that results in fundamental new science. And many scientists and engineers who work in what is considered to be pure research find very quickly that, once they have developed some new type of scientific knowledge, they are in an excellent position to apply it to commercial products. Many companies today employ scientists and engineers simply to explore new ideas, hoping that those new ideas will result in something that will eventually become useful. Many scientists who work on college campuses, where they teach as well as perform research, also have business relationships with high tech companies. For this reason, people rarely talk about themselves anymore as pure or applied scientists.

There is a fourth element to high technology, having to do with its commercial aspects, that wasn't mentioned above. High technology is inherently risky to the businesses that seek to use it and to the careers of the people who engage in it. A great number of new technologies that look extremely promising when first conceived never pan out. The company that invests in new technology can go bankrupt. The scientists and engineers, along with all the other company employees, can lose their jobs.

Don't let these facts scare you off from a high tech career—many other occupations have similar risks. Moreover, it is rare these days for new workers to join a company and then spend their entire career at that company. More often, professionals such as high tech workers move from one firm to another, gaining experience in a variety of industries. An academic posting at a college or university might also be a part of one's career.

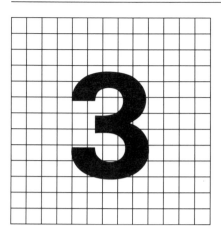

WHO ARE HIGH TECH WORKERS?

The next section of this book will provide details on the types of technologies and industries where high tech workers are employed. A more important classification for future high tech workers, though, is what types of professions are important. Once you have targeted a profession—even if you have only a hazy notion of where it might lead you—you can begin making preparations for college study.

THE NATURAL AND SOCIAL SCIENCES

High tech work, naturally enough, is dominated by the scientific and engineering professions. Among scientists, a distinction is usually made between the hard or natural sciences and the soft or social sciences. Examples of the former include geology, physics, biology, and chemistry; examples of the latter include psychology, sociology, and anthropology.

The hard sciences aren't so named because they are difficult to learn (although learning them is not very easy), but because they encompass subjects where experiments can be conducted and results obtained that represent a universal scientific truth. For example, a chemist can measure the atomic weight of an element, and that weight will be true for that element anywhere on Earth. The scientific knowledge has been reduced to "hard" numerical data.

In the social, or soft, sciences, experiments are conducted, but their results tend to be specific to one time and one place. A sociologist might measure the number of high-school dropouts in a city school system and attempt to account for the reasons teenagers have for not finishing school. That numerical data may change from year to year, however, and it certainly changes from one country to another. It is a "soft" result.

NATURAL SCIENCE AND ENGINEERING DISCIPLINES

Below is a list of the major natural sciences, based on the tabulation that the U.S. Department of Education uses when accounting for college graduations (academic departments in Canada are set up much the same way, although the overall number of graduates each year is far fewer than the number of U.S. grads).

Agricultural sciences (including animal and food sciences, soil science, and so on)
Biology
  Biochemistry
  Botany
  Cell and molecular biology
  Microbiology
  Ecology, marine biology, and other specialties
  Zoology
Computer and information sciences
Health sciences
  Nursing
  Pharmacy
  Pre-dentistry
  Pre-medicine
  Pre-veterinary
  Public health
Mathematics
  Pure and applied mathematics
  Statistics
Physical sciences
  Astronomy and astrophysics
  Atmospheric science
  Chemistry
  Earth science
  Geological sciences
  Physics

Another major grouping is the engineering disciplines. The U.S. Department of Education lists twenty-eight distinct engineering specialties, but the main groups are the following fourteen:

Aerospace
Agricultural
Bioengineering
Chemical
Civil, environmental, and architectural
Computer
Electrical and electronics
Engineering physics and mechanics

Geological
Industrial
Materials and metallurgical
Nuclear
Petroleum
Systems

The third major grouping is that of science and engineering technologies. Most of these disciplines parallel the same academic departments in the natural sciences or engineering, but the curriculum is quite different. The key groupings are as follows.

Architectural and civil
Electrical and electronics
Industrial production and manufacturing
Mechanical

Not all—or even most—scientists, engineers, and technologists work in high tech industries. And there are quite a few high tech workers who did not study these disciplines while in college. Nevertheless, these programs represent the core of the high tech workforce. High tech workers who are actively researching and developing the new technologies of tomorrow will either have college training in these disciplines or will have a good reason to account for why they don't.

NON-TECH WORKERS IN HIGH TECH

At this point, it is important to note that only part of the high tech workforce is comprised of professionals engaged in research and development. The annals of business history are filled with failed companies that had large staffs of top engineers and scientists, yet still went out of business because they were unable to commercialize or market a new technology. Today, additional types of professional experts are needed, especially in small, new firms trying to bring a new technology to the market.

These experts include lawyers (especially those experienced in patent law), sales and marketing professionals, communications experts (especially technical writers), business administrators, and human-resource managers. Usually, high tech industries hire people with liberal arts backgrounds for these types of jobs. A college graduate with a degree in, say, English or history will be challenged to learn about the technology that his or her employer is developing. The best ones will be able to cope with this challenge.

COLLEGE PREPARATION FOR HIGH TECH CAREERS

Alternatively, some students, and some employers, seek to cross this gap between the technical and the nontechnical by matching an undergraduate degree in some technical field with another degree. Some students carry a double major, such as business and engineering. This has the advantage of reducing the cost of higher education for the student by keeping the time necessary to gain both degrees to four or five years. It is, of course, a heavy load to carry during one's college years.

More commonly, students major in one program as an undergraduate and then study another discipline in graduate school. Some typical combinations are an undergraduate degree in engineering or science and a graduate degree in business. Technologist/lawyer is another combination. Some students go on to graduate school immediately after earning an undergraduate degree; others work for a few years in their chosen field before returning to the college campus. Yet others enter graduate programs in night school while holding down a daytime job.

A third course of action is to seek a cross-disciplinary major that offers exactly the combination one seeks. A close review of college catalogs reveals programs with names like "Technology and Public Policy" (great training for a career in a government research agency), "Technology Management," "Information Systems Management," "Communications Management" (that is, the combination of training in telecommunications and business management), and many others. The great majority of colleges in both the U.S. and Canada allow students to devise their own program of study, as independent majors, as long as certain academic standards are met. Generally speaking, these independent major programs work best for the students who know exactly what they want to do during their career. One drawback of such a tailored college education is that unless an employer is seeking just that combination of interests when the student graduates, a job may be hard to find.

One of the more exciting career endeavors these days, and one that is often best addressed by a cross-disciplinary degree, is environmental work. It is possible to study environmental engineering or natural resources programs such as forestry to gain a foothold in the booming environmental field. But the cross-disciplinary programs enable students to get a broader understanding of the environmental issues of the day and to make themselves more acceptable as job candidates to a wider range of employers.

As these options indicate, the challenge in preparing for a high tech career is not in finding the right program to study—there are so many options and so many strategies that the student can adopt. The real challenge is in making decisions about where one's interests lie. Keep in mind that the choices are yours.

Part Two
The High Tech
Industries

IDENTIFYING THE
HIGH TECH LIST

In this section, we'll take a brief look at some of the key industries that are engaged in high tech work. We'll walk around in their laboratories and factories and find out what goes on behind the glass and chrome doors in the futuristic buildings where many of these companies are headquartered. And we'll find out what kind of professionals are employed by these firms.

A point made in the preceding section bears repeating: There is no magic demarcation between high tech industry, low tech industry, or anything else. Even the most humdrum, traditional industries can undergo enormous changes as a new technical development makes old products and ways of doing things obsolete. When the new ways become accepted, an industry can rapidly join the high tech ranks.

This is not to say that all types of employers and all types of work are high tech. The industries that fall into the high tech ranks change over time, as technologies that were once new become the tradition. It is true, however, that the high tech workers tend to be the same kind: scientists, engineers, technologists, and businesspeople who are comfortable dealing with new technologies.

At the dawn of the 1990s, the high tech lineup includes business in space and under the oceans, in the complexities of computer circuitry, and in the intricacies of human biology. High tech industries are also a vitally important part of national economies—both in the United States and in Canada. The U.S. Department of Commerce, in an attempt to categorize high tech industries, identified business groups on the basis of the amount of money they spend on R&D. The average rate of increase of R&D spending by all businesses was in the neighborhood of 5.3 percent per year; high tech industries' rate of increase was 5.8 percent. "Other" manufacturing's rate of increase was 4.4 percent per year, and nonmanufacturing (services) increased by only 2 percent per year. On the basis of this comparison, the Department of Commerce has identified five major high tech sectors of the economy:

Chemicals and allied products
Machinery (including computers)
Electrical equipment
Aircraft and missiles
Professional and scientific instruments

Each of these sectors, in turn, has a few to a few dozen subcategories where technological developments are proceeding rapidly. A privately funded foundation, the U.S. Council on Competitiveness, has assembled another list of technologies that are labeled "critical" to the future well-being of the U.S. economy. These technologies are as follows:

I. Materials and Associated Processing Technologies
A. Advanced Structural Materials
  - Advanced metals, metal matrix composites, polymers, polymer matrix composites, structural ceramics

B. Materials Processing
  - Catalysts, chemical synthesis, membranes, net shape forming, precision coating, process controls

C. Electronic and Photonic Materials
  - Display materials, electronic ceramics, electronic packaging materials, gallium arsenide, magnetic materials, optical materials, photoresists, silicon, superconductors

D. Biotechnologies
  - Bioactive/biocompatible materials, bioprocessing, drug discovery techniques, genetic engineering

E. Environmental Technologies
  - Emissions reduction, recycling/waste processing

II. Engineering and Production Technologies
A. Design and Engineering Tools
  - Computer-aided engineering, human factors engineering, leading-edge scientific instruments, measurement technologies, structural dynamics, systems engineering

B. Commercialization and Production Systems
  - Computer-integrated manufacturing, design for manufacturing, design of manufacturing processes, flexible manufacturing, integration of research, design and manufacturing, total quality management

C. Process Equipment
* Advanced welding, high-speed machining, integrated circuit fabrication and test equipment, joining and fastening technologies, precision bearings, precision machining and forming, robotics and automated equipment

III. Electronic Components
A. Microelectronics
* Logic chips, memory chips, microprocessors, submicron technology

B. Electronic Controls
* Actuators, sensors

C. Optoelectronic Components
* Laser devices, photonics

D. Electronic Packaging and Interconnections
* Multichip packaging systems, printed circuit board technology

E. Displays
* Electroluminescent, liquid crystal, plasma and vacuum fluorescent

F. Hardcopy Technology
* Electrophotography, electrostatic

G. Information Storage
* Magnetic information storage, optical information storage

IV. Information Technologies
A. Software
* Applications software, artificial intelligence, computer modeling and simulation, expert systems, high-level software languages, software engineering

B. Computers
* Hardware integration, neural networks, operating systems, processor architecture

C. Human Interface and Visualization Technologies
* Animation and full-motion video, graphics hardware and software, handwriting and speech recognition, natural language, optical character recognition

D. Database Systems
* Data representation, retrieval and update, semantic modeling and interpretation

    E. Networks and Communications
- Broadband switching, digital infrastructure, fiber optic systems, multiplexing

    F. Portable Telecommunications Equipment and Systems
- Digital signal processing, spectrum technologies, transmitters and receivers

V. Powertrain and Propulsion Technologies
    A. Powertrain
- Alternative fuel engines, electric motors and drives, electrical storage technologies, high fuel economy/power density engines, low emission engines

    B. Propulsion
- Airbreathing propulsion, rocket propulsion

The common theme uniting these topics is that a panel of industry experts has agreed that these technologies are critical to the future well-being of the U.S. economy. The Council on Competitiveness went on to assess the current position of U.S. firms relative to foreign competitors relative to each of these technologies. In thirty-one of the technologies, the U.S. position was judged to be strong. In thirty of them, the assessment was competitive. In eighteen, the U.S. was weak. And in fifteen, the U.S. was "losing badly or lost." Which technologies are strong or weak isn't really important to our purposes here (in general, the engineering and production technologies are weak and certain of the electronic components technologies are weak or lost). What *is* important to note is that many companies and, to a lesser extent, the U.S. government have focused on these as areas where further development is desirable.

The remainder of this section will examine each of these categories. The types of innovations being developed will be reviewed, as well as the characteristics of employers in each of the fields. Finally, the job titles and working responsibilities will be explored.

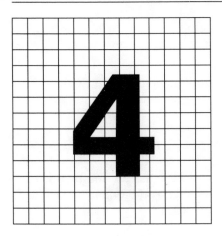

MATERIALS AND PROCESSING TECHNOLOGIES

"The New Alchemy" is the title that *Business Week* magazine recently used to describe the revolution going on in materials technologies. Alchemy, of course, was the search by scientists/magicians in medieval times to find a way to transmute base materials such as earth into gold. While this goal was never achieved, the ancient alchemists did develop many types of knowledge that later scientists were able to put to good use.

In this century, that age-old goal of transmuting materials became a reality with the dawn of the Atomic Age. Physicists who run large accelerators—machines that fire atoms against each other at high speeds—are able to combine atomic particles almost at will, turning one element into another. The catch is that this method of making a material like gold is much, much more expensive than digging it out of the ground.

Nevertheless, once scientists were able to devise tools for changing atoms or for directing them precisely to a specific location, a great variety of new applications opened up. For many such researchers, the model seems to replicate life itself—to be able to very accurately manufacture the molecules that make up muscles, bones, skin, and teeth. When you look at a microphotograph of, say, a leaf, the first thing you notice is the startling beauty of how cells interconnect with each other, and how they support the leaf's structure. If human researchers are able to replicate such detailed structures in an economical fashion, they have the potential of making better materials for everything from coffee cups to the struts that would support a Space Station.

THE MATERIALS

What are "materials"? They are the substances that are refined into some consistent form and content and then shaped into useful articles.

The traditional classes of materials are metals, ceramics, and fibers. Human civilization is partially defined by the movement from the Stone Age (stones are a type of ceramic) into a Bronze and Iron Age (both metals). Along the way, humans learned to take natural or refined materials and weave them into cloth or fabrics, which then made better clothing, housing, and transportation possible (what would an ancient ship be without its cloth sails?).

In this century, the big innovation was the development of synthetic polymers—plastics. A polymer is simply a long-chained string of atoms; when these strings are intertwined with each other, a durable yet flexible material is created. Some of the first polymers were developed to replace the fibers obtained from cotton or wool. By the 1940s and 1950s, scientists had learned how to manipulate polymers to create films (such as sandwich wrap) and solid sheets or blocks. The advantage of many of these polymers is that they can be molded easily and efficiently. To make a mental comparison, think about all the steps necessary in forming a metal cup (forming steel into a sheet, bending the sheet, welding it together somehow, and then bolting a handle onto it) versus making a plastic one (melting the plastic resin and then injecting it into a mold, from which the finished article pops out in a fraction of a second).

When engineers and other researchers began to experiment with plastics used in other applications, they quickly discovered a severe limitation of them. As a sheet or block of plastic gets larger, it becomes weaker. It flexes too much and is prone to cracking or warping under relatively low stresses. To get around this, researchers combined plastic resins with glass fibers to form a material we now commonly call fiberglass.

Fiberglass is valuable for applications where the weight of a structure is as important as its strength. These applications include aerospace vehicles, where fiberglass can be used for wings or body fuselages, and boat hulls. Fiberglass is a "composite" material, meaning simply that it is a combination of two or more different materials. As such, it can be considered to be one of the first modern high tech materials. Now fiberglass is commonly being used in automobiles or for housings for computers or other appliances. It is becoming a more common component of housing construction as well.

In recent years, the concept of a composite that combines the advantages of several different materials has become valuable in metals and ceramics. Countertops in kitchens are often a composite of plastic and clay or stone dust—a polymer/ceramic composite. Metals are being sintered (melted together) with ceramic powders—a metal/ceramic composite. Alternatively, a small amount of polymer is often added to concrete mixtures to strengthen them and make them resistant to chipping, a composite that is known as polycrete. Most recently, metallurgists have begun experimenting with mixing one type of metal with another (usually by mixing the two metal powders together and then firing the combination while it is being molded into the desired shape)—a metal matrix.

Some of these composite mixtures have the additional benefit that they can be easily molded—almost as easily as the original plastics were. This is called net shape forming, and it can greatly reduce the cost of machining, say, a toothed gear.

MATERIALS PROCESSING

The realm of materials processing includes a variety of highly specialized structures and compositions. In chemical manufacturing, these include catalysts, which are simply substances that speed up a chemical reaction, much as a jolt of adrenaline helps us run faster or harder. Catalysts are often a synthetic analog of a naturally occurring mineral; so catalyst research combines elements of geology and chemistry.

Another type of material often seen in chemical manufacturing is known as a membrane. These magical materials are usually constructed of polymeric plastics (although there are some ceramic membranes as well) that are fabricated in such a way that they have microscopically small pores in them. The pores are small enough to exclude some molecules, while allowing others to pass through unimpeded.

The commonest use of membranes is to desalinate seawater, making it drinkable. Vast networks of such membranes are now being used in the Middle East, where fresh water is scarce; they are also being considered for use in the drought-stricken regions of California. In industry, membranes are often used to separate air, splitting it into a stream of nearly pure nitrogen and another stream rich in oxygen. Previously, nitrogen was available only by chilling air to well below zero so that it liquefied; the nitrogen would freeze before the oxygen did, thus enabling a processor to separate the two. That process is still used, but it is highly energy-intensive and is economical only when large amounts are needed. With the new membrane-based systems, volumes of air small enough to run a food-processing shop (where the gas keeps food fresh) or for small-scale metal processing (to keep the metal from rusting and oxidizing while it is being processed) are now feasible.

Mention of below-zero temperatures brings to mind the famed warm superconductors—materials that can conduct electricity with no loss of energy. The property of superconductivity has been known since around the turn of the century, but has been possible only with exotic metals cooled to near absolute zero. The new superconductors are basically ceramics—mixtures of copper oxides with other minerals—sintered according to a highly specific formula. Instead of being chilled to near absolute zero, these new mixtures only need to be cooled to about $-280°F$, which is within the range of liquid nitrogen. When warm superconductors were initially developed, it was almost as if Superman's kryptonite had been found: People expected to have impossibly cheap energy and to ride monorails to the Moon overnight. Reality soon set in, and scientists are still carefully slogging through a thicket of knotty technical issues relating to the manufacture of large amounts of superconducting material. Good things are in store for warm superconductors, especially for microelectronic devices, and the rest may come in time.

ELECTRONIC MATERIALS

The microelectronic applications of materials technology are possibly the most exciting development of all. We have grown accustomed to seeing the luminescent displays of digital watches, which have been around for about twenty years. We are beginning to grow accustomed to so-called liquid crystal displays, such as are seen on many laptop personal computers and pocket televisions. Researchers in the U.S., Europe, and the Far East are striving energetically to adapt these technologies to large display screens, such as a desktop computer or even the biggest television sets. This display technology, which depends on sandwiching specialized chemicals between two glass sheets and then energizing them with light or electricity, may ultimately lead to a television set that is as big as a window and is mounted on the wall of a room.

That development could make watching soap operas from bed more convenient, but it could also help us in many more meaningful ways. A hospital could depend on such displays to help doctors and nurses monitor patients and to call up a patient's medical records quickly and easily. It could also improve the efficiency of television and video technology used in classrooms.

Another microelectronic compound that depends on new materials technologies is called gallium arsenide (a bonding of the elements gallium and arsenic). It has certain superior properties for the manufacture of microchips, polymer plastics that can conduct electricity, and the components of magnets and batteries.

WHO IS DOING R&D IN MATERIALS AND PROCESSES?

Who is carrying out all the R&D on new materials and processes? The answer depends on the specific application. In advanced metals and ceramics, the aerospace industry is the leader. Aerospace companies have explored all kinds of exotic metallurgies in the search for materials that can be used in high-speed, high-temperature jet turbines. They are also at the forefront of devising ultralight, yet ultrastrong structures, because every pound less of weight that a craft has translates into higher speed or better fuel efficiency. These aerospace firms hire materials scientists and mechanical and metallurgical engineers to carry out the research.

In the search for better catalysts, membranes, and related materials, the major chemical and petroleum producers have taken leadership positions. Mobil Oil, for example, developed a catalyst several years ago that functions well in transforming methanol, a small, one-carbon molecule, into gasoline, which is generally a many-carbon, long-chained molecule. Methanol-to-gasoline doesn't make sense economically except in those parts of the world where there is lots of natural gas (which is readily made into methanol) and little crude oil. New Zealand is one such place; eventually, due to heavy consumption, the United States will become such a place as well. Mobil's technology is already commercialized in New Zealand. In developing such technology, chemical and oil companies rely on chemists, chemical engineers, physicists, and instrumentation specialists.

The electronics applications of materials involve a wide range of companies, including small entrepreneurial outfits that are the brainchildren of one or two scientists, as well as the mighty computer and electronics manufacturers. It was at an IBM laboratory that warm superconductors were first conceived, and IBM has already succeeded in commercializing at least one electronic application of them.

BIOTECHNOLOGY

The Council on Competitiveness included biotechnology as one of the Materials and Associated Processing Technologies; this field has become a mighty industry that has developed its own patterns, successes, and markets. Biotech, to use the colloquial expression, arose in the 1970s out of the development of a series of unrelated techniques to examine and manipulate the basic genetic material of life. Two decades before, during the 1950s, biologists James Watson and Francis Crick verified the double-helix structure of deoxyribonucleic acid (DNA), which is the chemical name for basic genetic material. The fascinating thing about DNA is its combined simplicity and complexity. It is simple in that it is composed of only six subcomponents—a sugar molecule, a phosphate molecule, and four nitrogen compounds (adenine, thiamine, guanine, and cytosine). The sugar and phosphates form a backbone chain, and the four nitrogen compounds are distributed along this backbone. That's it. All the complexity of life, from a puny weed to the cells in our brains, is "written" in the four nitrogen bases.

The complexity of DNA arises from its minuscule size and the difficulty in transcribing this genetic code. DNA is millions of units long. Inside each cell, it resembles a tightly coiled snake. Simple chemical compounds are drawn out of the soup inside a cell and connected to each other according to the patterns defined by the four nitrogen bases. By the 1970s, a new research discipline, molecular biology, had arisen to address the daunting complexity of the DNA code. Molecular biologists figured out how to make DNA replicate its instructions, even when snipped from the original helix chain and transferred to another organism's DNA. Following another research path, molecular biologists succeeded in merging two cells together—one, a cancerous tumor cell (which has the unwholesome property of never "shutting off," but continuing to replicate), the other, a cell that produces a valued antibody (antibodies are chemicals that protect an organism from bacterial attack or other forms of infection). By combining the two, a fused cell known as a hybridoma is produced, which can produce the antibody practically without ever stopping. (As in all life, however, even a cell eventually dies.) These antibodies can be used to detect disease or even to combat it.

By about 1980, all the tools were in place for a veritable explosion of new biotechnology. Molecular biologists and biochemists were mixing many different types of DNA strands together, literally creating new forms of life. Antibodies that previously were obtained at fantastic expense and in minute supply could be produced in cookie-cutter fashion. Soon, some drugs and diagnostic compounds worth hundreds of millions of dollars were being produced. Among the products that have successfully been commercialized are human growth hormone (to counter the effects of dwarfism), tissue plasimogen activator (a compound that helps heart attack victims), and interferon (a potential cancer fighter). Today, too, a woman can perform a pregnancy test quickly and inexpensively in her own home with a pregnancy test kit that has its roots in antibody R&D.

All these products are geared toward human health and needs. A similar revolution is brewing in plant and animal science, where age-old diseases are being combatted and where new, hardier crops are being developed. Historically, plant and animal scientists could develop a better crop or farm animal only by patiently crossing and recrossing breeds of them to bring forth new generations of life forms with the desired properties. Now, by manipulating genetic material, these properties can be targeted and expressed directly and quickly.

A variety of new professions have arisen due to the emergence of biotechnology. Many of these are at the leading edges of biological research. For instance, molecular biologists are able to analyze genetic material molecule by molecule and to manipulate the genetic material with other chemicals. The types of biotechnological applications that are emerging call for specialization even within molecular biology. There are protein chemists and biologists (proteins make up our muscles and tissues; DNA is a protein); enzymologists (enzymes control body chemistry); endocrinologists (who focus on hormones); immunologists (the immune system of the body combats illness); and virologists (who work with viruses). The dreadful loss of life caused by the AIDS virus in the past decade has intensified the search for new biotechnological answers, including a vaccine for the disease.

The recent history of biotechnology is not one of uniform success. Many companies tried and failed to commercialize techniques that either didn't produce the desired result or were felt to be too risky. In addition, the early forecasts of cranking out large volumes of hormones or other biochemicals for humans by genetically engineering bacteria have been tempered by the realizations that many biochemicals have other levels of complexity that scientists were only dimly aware of. The three-dimensional structure of biochemicals is an example of this; it is not enough to make a chemical with all the right molecules in a row; this chemical must also have the right spatial arrangement in order to function properly.

Still, thousands of biologists, biochemists, food and agriculture scientists, and others have joined the hundreds of new companies that have arisen in the past fifteen years to commercialize biotechnology. Year by year, the list of products that have been introduced lengthens, and more will come.

ENVIRONMENTAL TECHNOLOGY

The last area of technology specified by the Council on Competitiveness in the materials and processing area is environmental technology. Environmental protection and remediation has been one of the hot fields of the 1980s and 1990s. People talk about "green" marketing of environmentally friendly goods; cities announce new recycling initiatives to cut the flow of garbage pouring into city dumps; international diplomats gather to agree on regulations to protect the Earth's atmosphere from harmful chemical pollution.

At first glance, many people would believe that environmental protection and job generation are opposites: when one goes up, the other goes down. It has been true in the past that, when a factory was threatened with a shutdown due to uncontrolled pollution, jobs were at stake. But in the intervening years, industry has learned not only that environmental protection preserves the capital invested in factories, but also that it makes eminently good business sense to be a better environmental performer. And for the rare business manager who wants to continue to pollute, regardless of the consequences, the U.S. Environmental Protection Agency now has an offer that cannot be refused: jail time.

In truth, few business managers ignore environmental issues. The great need, however, is to develop technologies that reduce or eliminate wastes and pollution without driving a company to the brink of financial ruin. The need is especially acute in facing the problem of air pollution and in dealing with old chemical dumps that dot the countryside. Once the toxic chemicals that are inevitably present in municipal garbage get dumped, they can seep through the ground and contaminate drinking wells, schools, and homes.

A large number of companies, especially in the engineering consulting field, have arisen over the past decade to address these environmental issues. The specialty profession of hydrogeology (the study of water in soil) has become critical to cleanup projects. A great number of civil engineers are devoted to building new waste treatment facilities and to providing fresh drinking water and decontaminated sewage water. Chemical engineers are employed by most chemical manufacturers to review production processes, looking for ways to cut wastes and noxious byproducts.

According to Management Information Services, a Washington, D.C., consulting group, environmental spending in the United States is currently running at a rate of $129 billion a year. By the year 2005, spending on pollution abatement and control (PABCO) will total $240 billion (in 1991 dollars) annually, while spending for national defense will slide to $200 billion. "This is a momentous development," says James Easterly, an executive with Management Information Services. "An entire economic sector [defense] was created and nurtured—as were many large and profitable companies and millions of jobs—for more than forty years. Within a decade this 'engine' of the economy will be eclipsed by the PABCO industry."

Management Information Services further concludes that there are already 3.5 million jobs dependent on PABCO. If the number of jobs doubles over the next fifteen years, as spending is expected to, there will be over 7 million jobs devoted to the field.

As with electronics or biotechnology, there are both large, old-time corporations and new, startup companies engaged in environmental protection. Some of the consulting firms that have matured over the past decade have gone from a handful of employees to staffs in the thousands in offices spanning the globe. Some chemical companies, such as DuPont, have set up environmental services divisions to parlay the experience they have gained in dealing with their own pollution problems into profit centers. DuPont expects such a division in its corporate body to grow from $100 million in sales currently to over $1 billion by the end of the decade.

Many environmental problems are a matter of stopping questionable industrial or social practices, such as dumping sludge in the ocean or allowing chemical companies to discard untreated waste chemicals in landfills. But many others are extremely complex challenges that test existing technology. New, high technology solutions are required.

A case in point is the cleanup of contaminated groundwater. When toxic chemicals percolate through the ground after they are dumped, they don't simply disappear. As water wells are dug, or as the natural movement of water through the ground occurs, these chemicals re-emerge, making water undrinkable and killing off wildlife in lakes. There are a variety of techniques being used to correct this problem; one is to pump genetically selected microorganisms into the site of the underground contamination, along with a source of oxygen (such as the chemical hydrogen peroxide, which gives off oxygen) and the appropriate nutrients to maintain the organisms. The goal is to establish a colony of microbes that will digest the offending chemicals.

For heavily contaminated soil near the surface, one technique being tested is to irradiate the soil with high doses of microwave energy. The radiation breaks down the chemicals and solidifies the soil, reducing the amount of leaching-out of the contaminants.

Still other environmental issues are improved by the use of some of the high tech materials mentioned earlier. For example, a fairly common problem in industry is large volumes of water that have exceedingly small—but still dangerous—levels of contamination. The water could be boiled to drive off the contaminant, but that is energy-intensive and expensive. An alternative is to use membranes (such as are used to desalinate water) to filter the contaminant out.

Air pollution is a monumental worry for industry, especially in the wake of the revised Clean Air Act, which was passed in late 1990 by the U.S. Congress. Among other things, this law mandates reductions in sulfur compounds in the air, the source of acid rain that is of great concern to both the United States and Canada.

Another problem that the Clean Air Act addresses is the generation of nitrogen oxides, which can generate acidic compounds in the air and are harmful (in high concentrations) to human lungs. To minimize nitrogen oxide generation, the operators of power-generating furnaces and other combustion devices must minimize the amount of air (which is mostly nitrogen) passing through the furnace. But air, of course, is essential to combustion because it also provides the oxygen that allows combustion to continue. One way to deal with this dilemma is to provide high-powered computer controls on the furnace that can sense the energy content of the incoming fuel precisely and adjust the airflow to suit it. Another method is to attempt to remove the nitrogen oxides after they are formed through some sort of scrubbing system that purifies the exhaust gases. These scrubbers often use specialized catalysts combined with neutralizing compounds.

Recycling has become a new growth industry throughout North America, especially in regions with heavy waste-disposal burdens, such as New York, California, New England, and Ontario. Recycling is not new, nor is it necessarily high tech: the junkyard and the auto scrap yard have been an element of the economy for decades. Still, there are many new issues being confronted by recyclers as they seek to address wastes that heretofore have not been recycled.

A good example of this is recycled plastics. Theoretically, there is nothing that prevents the recycling of most plastics; they do not "wear out" with use (although the products made with them do break down in time, as do most other materials). Practically, though, the problems of cleaning a used plastic article sufficiently and of preventing the contamination of one type of plastic with another are serious limitations. Most plastics today are ground up and melted together, regardless of the type of plastics contained, and this limits the resale value. GE Plastics, a major producer of so-called engineering resins used in many automotive applications, may have some solutions to this problem. GE Plastics' products are all thermoplastics. This means that they can be liquefied and remolded simply by heating them sufficiently (other plastics decompose before they melt). By carefully selecting the types of resins that are used in, for instance, the bumper and headlight assembly of a car, an auto manufacturer enables the auto recycler to remove the entire assembly, which can then be sent off to be recycled into a new product. GE Plastics has also built a home of the future near Springfield, Massachusetts, to showcase how recycled materials could be successfully used in construction applications, ranging from plastic "bricks" that are as strong as cement ones, yet light enough to be carried and positioned quickly to networks of pipes and wiring conduits that can be snapped together, rather than glued or welded.

There are many other environmental issues that will call for the expertise of well-trained scientists and technologists in the future. The growth in environmental spending and the strength of public demand for improvement will see to that. Moreover, most existing types of manufacturing and common social activities, such as automotive or aircraft transportation, housing, and recreation, will require steady improvement in amount of environmental impact.

As things stand today, civil and environmental engineering are the most direct beneficiaries of the heightened environmental awareness. Chemical, mechanical, and electrical engineers are also getting involved. On the life sciences side, most biology-based disciplines can find an environmental component. These include agricultural sciences and each of the biology specialties connected with the various forms of life (ichthyology for fish, ornithology for birds, entomology for insects, and so on). Chemists, geologists, and physicists are involved in earth sciences, atmospheric research, natural-resource development, and water management.

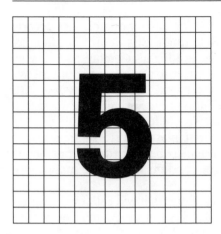

ENGINEERING AND PRODUCTION TECHNOLOGIES

There are two main themes to advances in manufacturing technology today: the increased use of automation technologies, involving nearly every aspect of computers, and the drive to improve product quality through such techniques as total quality management (TQM).

About the time that the phrase "high technology" came into common use in the late 1970s there was a decided bias against low tech businesses, including the basic manufacture of materials, machines, automobiles, and the like. Most of these longer-lived technologies were lumped together as smokestack industries (a smokestack being the most common visual element that tied all of them together), and many people felt that throughout North America, smokestack industries would fade away to more distant countries and that the more technology-intensive industries like electronics, aerospace, and biotechnology would remain and would replace what had been lost.

For a while, it looked as if all this was true, but during the early 1980s, a severe recession gripped the continent, and old-line manufacturers across the land were decimated. Many steel companies, oil producers, metal fabricators, and chemical manufacturers went out of business or were absorbed by still-healthy firms. But then a striking realization gripped the remaining manufacturers: they were in a fight for their economic lives, and even if the majority of the population did not depend on them for employment, they were still the wellspring out of which all wealth in the land arose.

As the recession ended and both the United States' and Canada's economy came roaring back, manufacturers felt a sense of rebirth. They could compete with newer, lower-cost manufacturers from abroad by investing in the latest technology and by running their factories more intelligently. An essential ingredient in that better management was the use of updated, modernized techniques. This updating is still going on.

A good example of more intelligent manufacturing is a type of analysis of manufacturing known as statistical process control (SPC). When mass-production factories are in operation, it is common for the output to be examined by quality control experts to make sure that the products meet their specifications and do not vary significantly from one batch to the next. In the past, this had been done after the products were made. Learning from the Japanese, however (and such American experts as W. Edward Deming), manufacturers realized that it is much more effective to monitor quality while the products are being made, rather than afterwards. And the best way to do this is to apply the mathematics of statistics to the production process, measuring variations—no matter how minute—in each product and making sure that something that is only slightly off-spec now doesn't become seriously out of spec at a later point. Thus, SPC.

To run SPC properly, large amounts of data must be gathered rapidly on a variety of product characteristics. These data must be compared, and calculations must be made as to variations. Then, a manufacturing manager must pinpoint problem areas and see to it that the problems are resolved. All this must happen quickly, while production is ongoing, so that final product quality is maintained at an elevated level. Such an application calls for computers in large numbers.

But the problem is more complex than simply positioning many computers throughout the factory floor and pouring in production data. Elaborate software programs must be available to automate the data-gathering and analysis steps. When a problem is encountered, the computer system must be able to isolate it and indicate what countermeasures should be taken. Finally, it is increasingly common for all the final product specifications to be delivered along with the product itself, especially in cases where the output of one manufacturer (a steel company, for example) goes to another manufacturer (an appliance supplier). There are new national and international standards to be met in supplying these data.

The bottom line for engineers and scientists is that there are plenty of high-tech opportunities for supplying these programs and computerized analyses to even decidedly low-tech forms of manufacturing. Some of these technologists are employed by the manufacturers themselves; others are employed by consulting organizations that are hired by the manufacturers for their expertise.

WHO WORKS WITH AUTOMATION TECHNOLOGIES?

Industrial engineering is one profession whose employment prospects are dramatically affected by automation technology. It used to be that industrial engineers were employed primarily to figure out the most efficient use of human labor (by measuring, for example, how long it took a worker to perform a certain task). Today, however, the industrial engineer looks at the total manufacturing process.

Another specialized profession that influences factory automation and quality control is called operations research. Operations researchers are trained to analyze complex tasks with sophisticated mathematical techniques. The profession originated in the needs of the military during World War II to figure out the best ways of providing armed forces in the field with necessary supplies. In peacetime, it was applied to the needs of airlines (which have to make sure that airplanes are in the right locations at all times), telecommunications systems, and, ultimately, factories. As with the industrial engineer, the computer is an essential tool for the operations researcher.

Along with new attention being paid to how factory operations are organized and run, high tech workers are also examining typical manufacturing processes to uncover improvements. These include such basic tasks as bending or cutting metal with complex machine tools. Metal can be cut (or joined) by hot torches (or welding machines); the use of high-temperature plasma torches is one example of how a traditional operation has been updated. (A plasma is a stream of hot, electrically charged matter; the sun, for example, is mostly plasma.)

In the early 1980s, robotics captured the attention of the public and manufacturing researchers alike. A robot is essentially a computer-controlled device that carries out a complex task. There were estimates that robotics would become a new type of business worth tens of billions of dollars. The experience of most manufacturers, however, is that the benefits of robots were greatly overstated. They are useful for certain limited tasks, such as conveying inventory parts around the factory floor. But they have not proved to be better than the combination of a well-trained worker using modern, efficient machines and tools. When robots do perform better, many manufacturers discovered that the robot was too expensive to justify replacing the worker/machine combination.

Robotics continues to be important, and a considerable number of mechanical and electrical engineers, along with computer scientists, are employed in developing and using robots.

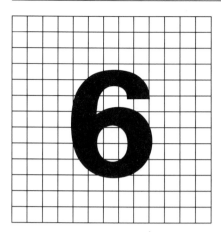

ELECTRONIC COMPONENTS

There is little doubt that the computer (and all the associated electronics and software) has brought about the most fundamental changes in modern society. From how we do business to how we entertain ourselves to how we keep in touch with each other, computers, microchips, and software have transformed our world.

To people untrained in computer use or construction, computers remain something of a frightening prospect. This fear is usually overcome by familiarity, and few people working with computers every day and becoming aware of all their shortcomings remain intimidated. Yet this fear is proof of the influence the computer has over our everyday lives. It is also a testament to the problems that still remain inherent in computers for many people: they are hard to understand, difficult to use, and still, a good thirty years after their introduction, foreign to human experience.

The overall computer equipment market is about $75 billion annually, according to data cited by the U.S. Department of Commerce. An additional $30 billion or so is spent on computer software. The revenues of companies that provide information services based on computers adds another $100 billion. This brings the total to well over $200 billion. At least one million workers are employed in computer manufacture, software development, and computerized information services.

As these figures indicate, there is at least as much money, if not more, spent on the *use* of computers as on their manufacture. This has been true for many years. The typical concept has been of a young person eager to work in computers becoming a computer designer or manufacturer, preferably at an industry leader such as IBM. Yet an equally high tech career can be found in producing information via computers, from the daily financial data that Wall Street depends on to the CD-ROM disks that provide the text of a report or book at the user's desktop.

The computer industry sometimes reminds one of Texans, who are famous for bragging about nearly anything. Case in point: Most businesses are happy to grow consistently at a rate slightly above the overall growth in the Gross National Product (GNP), a measure of the size of the overall economy. In most years, that rate would be in the range of 4 to 8 percent. Computer manufacturers, on the other hand, consider any growth rate below 10 percent to be a slump. For example, a couple of years ago David Kearns, the chairman of Xerox Corporation, was interviewed by the *Wall Street Journal*. He "leaves no doubt that [the company will] return to the double-digit growth rates it last saw in the mid-1980s, 'rather than dinking along at 6 percent or 7 percent.' "

There are two great divisions in the world of computers: hardware and software. Usually, hardware is the realm of engineers, especially electrical and computer engineers. In software, the dominant type of academic training is computer science. But because there are so many professionals concerned with different types of applications of computers, there are many other types of academic training for software development as well, including information science, management of information systems (MIS), data processing, and computer programming. And because of the new emphasis on personal computers and computer graphics, a variety of professions that combine artistic skills with computing are coming to the fore. These include graphics designer, CAD (computer aided design) engineering, desktop publishing, and computer visualization. As the following discussion will show, many other types of technical degrees are employed in the manufacture and use of computers and information systems.

One further general comment is in order before the specific technologies of the computer world are reviewed. It has already been noted that high technology is inherently risky; high tech workers are at the forefront of their fields, and very often the applications they are developing never become successful. This is certainly true in the computer world. A successful new technology roars like wildfire through the field, turning a small company into a giant almost overnight. But a failed technology dies almost as quickly. Companies that make a wrong turn in rolling out a new product or that stumble in demonstrating the reliability and usefulness of a new technology fade in a hurry.

In the early 1990s, the computer business found itself in a slump. Sales of existing products had reached a plateau, and the new products that the industry put forward had not yet won wide acceptance. Computer manufacturers continually look for what's called the "killer app," short for killer application. This refers to a new program or application that suddenly becomes cost-effective for a large number of users, resulting in an explosion of sales for the computers and associated software. This is what happened in the early days of personal computers (PCs) when the spreadsheet program Lotus 1-2-3 appeared. In the mid-1980s, the widespread availability of CAD software made a type of computer called the engineering workstation very common. New "apps" appear regularly in the computer field, but it is next to impossible to predict from what direction the next innovation will come.

ELECTRONIC DEVICES

The Council on Competitiveness composed an extensive list of electronic devices that deserve closer attention in the future. These include microprocessors (the brains of any computer), memory chips, sensors, printed circuit boards, and printing devices. New data-storage techniques, using magnetic or optical phenomena, are also on the priority list.

All these developments share a dependence on new materials processing technologies. Some of them are truly amazing: the fine lines that connect components on a microchip, for example, are now less than a half-micron wide, which is hundreds of times thinner than a human hair. Researchers both in the U.S. and in Japan are using electron beams to etch lines so small they can only be seen in a high-powered microscope.

However, new materials science is not the only path to innovation in electronics. Determining how best to organize those lines and devices into a powerful microprocessor opens new vistas. For the engineering workstation and PC markets, for example, there is a new organizational method to the microprocessor called reduced instruction-set computing, or RISC. An instruction set is the combination of an electronic component and an order to perform a task, such as adding to multiplying an electric signal. Conventional microchips have complex instruction sets, with techniques for assembling and ordering data that are important. RISC throws out most of these conventions and emphasizes having a microchip that can perform a limited number of logical steps before the signal is sent along to the next chip or data container. What the RISC chip lacks in complexity it makes up in power—the simplified circuit architecture allows it to execute instructions rapidly. It is for reasons like these that RISC chips are now showing up in all sorts of computers, from PCs to minicomputers.

There are two things that more powerful microchips allow electronics designers to do: make equipment smaller, and obtain it for much less expense. When a component becomes less expensive, the designer has the option of loading more features into a product. Because of the miniaturization of microchips, even something like an auto engine now has a computer chip on it (imagine trying to encase a PC inside an engine compartment and you can see why this has not been possible before). And because of the reduced cost, many operations that were outside the budgets of most people are now very much within the realm of possibility.

A good example of this is desktop publishing. Even when the first personal computers were marketed, along with simple printing devices, hardly anyone could produce a finished document suitable for distributing or selling. To produce a high-quality document, computer users of the early 1980s were advised to take their computer files to a printer, who could then typeset it and reprint it. But with the passage of about seven years, laser printers became available. (One attribute of most laser printers is the inclusion of a microprocessor, so that the printer is itself a computer.) At the same time, the existence of high-quality printers motivated software developers to write programs that could generate the eye-pleasing typefaces that readers demand. In order to sell this software widely, the software developers were also dependent on computer designers who were packing much more memory and data-storage capacity into their computer boxes. The result: For a relatively small expense, a small business or individual can now publish books, magazines, or newsletters or can compose advertisements and similarly highly designed documents with a PC.

A nearly identical story can be told in a different medium—music. With the adoption of communication rules and new electronics, a composer can now write a musical piece at a PC. The sounds of the appropriate instruments can be synthesized electronically, and even the recording can be produced with music-editing hardware. A musician can now orchestrate, perform, and produce finished music from a room in his or her own house.

WHAT LIES AHEAD?

That's the recent history of computers. Now let's consider what might lie in the very near future. The most immediate development will be the combination of written documents, graphic images, and sound—a technology called multimedia computing. There are multimedia products available today, but at relatively high expense. The day is not far off, however, when an individual will be able to combine a high-quality television monitor with a state-of-the-art stereo and the newest PCs to take a self-guided tour through the world's museums or to learn Canadian history while listening to the actual voices of the leaders of the past and viewing the documents and events of earlier eras.

If you can conceive, in a simplified way, of the amount of information that must be converted into electronic signals and then sent down a transmission line to a display monitor or stereo speaker, you can readily see that providing the capacity to carry this information must get larger. This is a serious problem for a wide variety of communication media, including telephones, computer communications, television, and radio. Each of these media has been assigned a portion of the electromagnetic spectrum (the spectrum of force emanations that range from light in all its colors, radio waves, "short" waves, microwaves, up to X-rays and other emanations that carry high amounts of energy). The problem is that while the various communication media are increasing, the physical spectrum cannot—it is what it is, defined by the physical universe around us.

Dealing with this issue is the realm of the communication technologies, which include electronics, physics, and material sciences. The problems are complex because if one communications medium overlaps with another, an interference is created that affects both. People who hear local police-band radio transmissions over their radio are already familiar with the problem. In many telecommunications systems, interference caused by anything from solar flares on the surface of the sun to electrical storms are a continual worry.

High technology comes to the rescue in the form of optical communications. Light travels faster than electricity (usually) and can also carry much more information in a single slice of time than an electrical signal can. Yet another advantage of optical communications is that it is impervious to electrical interference caused by machines or lightning. By using fiber optics, computers are able to transmit vastly increased data over communication lines that stretch for miles. Today, it is common to have fiber optic connections within an office building and sometimes within neighboring buildings. These are called local area networks (LANs). In the near future, this technology will be extended to entire cities (MANs, or municipal area networks) and ultimately geographical regions (WANs, or wide area networks). Today, where a typical household has a telephone line, a cable television line, and radio and TV antennas, the future may bring one line that carries all these media.

In some cities, it is not uncommon to see someone walking down the street, talking into a hand-held telephone. This is cellular telephone technology, and it entails the creation of local radio "cells" (each one covering a few city blocks) that pick up the radio transmission, switch into a conventional telephone network, and convey the transmission to the other party on the line. It is expensive, but very convenient relative to the already existing telephone system. Now picture such a network in a Third World country lacking any telephone equipment at all. Instead of going through the years of work and millions of dollars of investment, many of these cities can establish a telephone network by using cellular telephone technology. Its introduction will be a tremendous boost for the local economies in much of the Third World. In this case, the advent of new technology will help underdeveloped countries leapfrog over much of the Industrial Revolution, entering the twenty-first century with the same tools as the developed countries.

In a different context, electronics and communications technologies will help the physically challenged. The speech-impaired today are able to communicate with specialized telephones that enable conversation to be written rather than spoken. Those with hearing difficulties are getting improved hearing-aid devices. Some attempts have been made to implant an electronic link in damaged nervous systems, so that hearing can be improved, or, with the right computer control, those with spinal injuries can attempt to walk. The technology is primitive, but the same advantages that electronic technology brings to other applications—miniaturization and lower cost—may someday bring nearly complete powers to the handicapped.

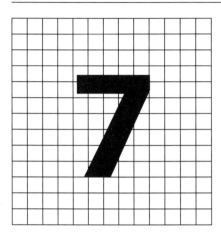

INFORMATION TECHNOLOGIES

One of the curious things about the early days of the computer era was that no one knew how to write programs or how to train people to write programs. Mathematicians and other scientists had many insights, but there were other professionals who made significant contributions with everything from music to language arts backgrounds. Even today, in some very advanced situations, such nontechnological professions as anthropology, philosophy, art, and psychology are influencing the direction of computer technology.

The reason for this is simple: No matter how much hardware is hooked up, at some point a computer has to interact with a human being. The human may be a programmer or operator, the audience of a multimedia presentation, or a student benefiting from computer-aided instruction. At this interface between human and machine, all the knowledge of humans and human thought becomes as important as the knowledge of electronic circuits, physics, and mechanics.

Nevertheless, in most common situations today, it is the computer professional who writes the instructions that guide a computer. The usual degree for this work is computer science. Related disciplines include computer engineering and information technology.

COMPUTER LANGUAGES

It was in the early 1960s, when the first high-powered, general-purpose computers came into being, that scientists stopped talking about computer instructions and began speaking of computer languages. The metaphor is an absolutely correct one—computer languages *are* a language, with a grammar and specific ways of expressing thoughts or actions and asking questions.

The earliest languages were called machine languages, because they were structured very much as a machine would operate. Each step in a process was carefully encoded. A sample might read, "Take entry A. Move to register 1. Take entry B. Move to register 2. Add registers 1 and 2. Store result in register 3. Take register 3 and print as entry C." All this is simply to say, "add A and B and display result as C." Newer languages did not evolve out of new computer hardware, but rather out of new ways of organizing thoughts and expressions. Because the logic of mathematics was the model for many of these languages, mathematicians had special insights into the process, as they do today. With the next stage of evolution, languages became user friendly. A person could write a program using simple English-language instructions. Then, another program kicks in—an interpreter that takes the instructions and translates them into machine language. Machine language is still in common use today, but is rarely seen by the computer operator, only by the computer.

Nevertheless, computer programming is still difficult. The ultimate evolution of computer languages and interpretation will be natural language programming, through which the operator will simply talk to the computer, and the instructions will be translated automatically into a computer version.

COMPUTER PROGRAMMING

Once languages are in place, it becomes obvious that there is something to do with them—write a program. Again, the metaphor of language is appropriate. Just as a poet, novelist, or teacher uses language to write a poem, novel, or textbook, so a computer programmer can use language to write some useful or entertaining program that the computer is guided by. How many programs are there in existence today? They must number in the millions. Hundreds of main programs have thousands of subprograms, and many standard programs are now capable of being customized by their users into specialized programs.

In the business world, one of the most widely used programs is called a database management system, or DBMS. A database is simply a collection of facts, usually with some relationship among them. A telephone directory is a database, as is a dictionary. A bank, for example, might take a database of its customers, listing their names, addresses, accounts, and preferences for investment or saving. Then, when a new type of savings account is to be marketed, the bank will create a mailing list of its customers and send introductory letters to those who would be interested in that type of account.

A more challenging DBMS for a bank (and many other business organizations) is a real-time database—one whose information is current up to the last minute. This type of program is necessary for a bank that has cash machines: The machine must gain near-instant access to a checking account, subtract the amount of money the customer wants, and update the account record so that the account cannot be overdrawn by subsequent withdrawals. This might seem a trivial task, one that is normally taken care of by tellers at bank windows. Nevertheless, it makes a tremendous difference in terms of the convenience of the bank's services to customers and the cost of banking itself.

Nor is such a DBMS so trivial when one considers an air traffic control system. In this case, lives are at stake in keeping the system up to date for the position and condition of aircraft circling an urban airport. Air traffic controllers find that their constant vigilance is helped by having a high-speed, real-time DBMS to monitor.

A DBMS is just one example of a useful computer program. Other widely used programs are for word processing, numerical analysis (such as a spreadsheet), drawing, making graphs or other numerical representations, education, or mechanical or construction design. One of the most exciting new types of programming is for writing software itself—a field called computer-aided software engineering (CASE).

CASE will become a $5 billion market by the mid-1990s, according to market analysts cited in a recent issue of *IEEE Spectrum,* the monthly journal of the Institute for Electrical and Electronics Engineers in Washington, D.C. Simply put, CASE helps to automate the process of writing software. Notwithstanding the strides that have been made in making computer languages easier to read and write, it is still a time-consuming, expensive task. And once a program is written, it must usually be updated or maintained, which means that a company that buys a large, expensive program must also purchase the time of experts knowledgeable in the program to keep it performing well.

CASE, it is hoped, will improve the efficiency of writing software, leaving more time available for software engineers to develop other programs or to explore new ways of developing the programs they are most involved with. (A constant problem of many software engineers is that they may be very well versed in computer technology, but relatively uninformed about the applications for which they are writing a program. By spending more time with the users of such programs, the engineer may be better equipped to provide the appropriate software.)

A key component in CASE is a form of computer languages known as object-oriented programming, or OOP. OOP is difficult to explain without being knowledgeable about computer programming itself, but it can be likened to a hardware store where many different tools are stored. When a carpenter needs to start a project, he or she is likely to need hammers, saws, power tools, and supplies. In a similar manner, the computer programmer using OOP will take a variety of "objects"—tool-like components of a program—and assemble them into the program that is needed.

ARTIFICIAL INTELLIGENCE

CASE and OOP use the inherent power of computers to assist the programmer. What if one were to let the computer itself do the programming? This raises the subject of artificial intelligence, the term used to describe the ability (or even existence) of a computer to think for itself. Artificial intelligence, or AI, has been the subject of innumerable science fiction stories, especially ones where a human-like robot is equipped with an AI "brain"—an artificial person!

It is not impossible to imagine that something like this may come in the distant future, when robotics, programming, and computer technology have all advanced dramatically. But in the meantime, there are a number of more mundane applications where AI technology is being developed and used. The most common one is expert systems, which encode a set of rules in a logical order so that a computer can predict a condition or situation on the basis of previous experience. (The name comes from the practice of interviewing a human expert about some situation and then taking those responses and transforming them into computer code.) A relatively simple example of expert systems technology is the "help" screen that comes up on a PC whenever the user is stuck on a procedure. Based on past experience, the expert system "knows" what the likely problems are for the user and can thereby provide useful assistance.

Other examples of AI programming are speech recognition (that is, understanding spoken words that are automatically converted into digital electronic signals), machine vision, the above-mentioned CASE, and automated machine control. The newest twist to AI research is the development of neural networks; these have nothing to do with LANs or WANs, but rather refer to a computer program modeled after the interconnections in an animal brain. According to biological researchers, individual brain cells—neurons—do not each remember a single fact or hold a single logical action, but rather work in concert with other neurons. The old expression "the whole is greater than the sum of its parts" applies here. In computer programming, the neural network represents a program that has subcomponents that can be made to "learn" from prior experience. Thus, by running the program through a series of repetitive actions, the program becomes more powerful. The field is still deep in the research phase, but prospects look good.

There are two ways of looking at the success of AI work. On the one hand, there have been many successful commercial applications, such as expert systems and machine vision. These are already woven into the design of many other computer programs. In another context—such as natural language programming or neural networks—the field is still being debated by researchers, with some expressing doubts that any commercial product will ever be developed. These AI researchers work in academia and in the basic research laboratories of leading computer manufacturers and software developers.

WHO WORKS IN INFORMATION TECHNOLOGIES?

In the larger world of computer manufacture, telecommunications services, software, and computer services, there are several types of employers. Both the large telecommunications firms and the computer makers tend to have large staffs of programmers and systems analysts (a managerial title for many computer workers) who work on the in-house computing needs of their employers. Many computer manufacturers find it essential for the successful marketing of their products to have prepackaged programs available for use by their customers. There are a handful of large software houses—Microsoft Corp. being the largest one—that offer a variety of programs to be used on a variety of computers. In the computer-user community, there are a large number of consulting organizations whose task is basically to go into a client company to systematize and overhaul existing computer resources in order to establish procedures and standards. Finally, there is a truly enormous number of small software companies, ranging from one to a few dozen employees, that write specialized software. These programs are sometimes used by the larger software houses or computer manufacturers. One of the wondrous aspects of the computer business is that, if you have a good idea, you can write a program and attempt to sell it through a variety of marketing channels that have been organized for just that purpose. If your idea flies, the product could become exceedingly successful in a short period of time.

Software writers do not work in a vacuum—they must be able to coordinate their activities with computer makers (who establish the framework under which a program can be run) and other software companies whose products may dominate a section of the marketplace. It is for this reason that the subject of standards and protocols becomes important. There is a very natural desire on the part of both software writers and users to organize programs that use standardized procedures and that work as well on one "platform" (type of computer) as another. At the same time, software developers seek to differentiate themselves from their competitors, so they load all sorts of proprietary features that other programs lack. The software world has become more predictable as standards get established, but new types of knowledge in computer programming continue to expand nonetheless.

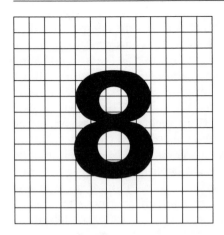

POWERTRAIN AND PROPULSION TECHNOLOGIES

The final area of technology concentration of the Council of Competitiveness is essentially that of transportation and power. A powertrain is the machinery that makes an automobile or truck go. Electrical or chemical energy is transformed to a moving shaft, which can be used to turn wheels. A propulsion system uses fuel or other forms of energy directly to provide forward momentum—as is the case of a jet airplane or a rocket.

CREATING AND GENERATING POWER

One interesting aspect of both these areas is that the same general types of devices that use fuel to *create* power can also be used to *generate* power (usually in the form of electricity) by causing a mechanical device to rotate in an electrical field (the basic attribute of turbines or other types of power generators). Thus, the investigation of new motors or other motion devices is also the investigation of the generation of power.

Going faster through distance has been *the* objective of technology since before the Industrial Revolution in the 1800s. The first mechanical engines ran on steam, and these engines had the distinction of helping formulate the first scientific laws of energy and energy transformation. They were followed by the internal combustion engines that drove automobiles and ships, and then airplanes, farm tractors, and trucks—all the vehicles we have today. In each transportation sector, whether by land, sea, or air, research continues on engines, motors, and other drive mechanisms.

One of the more exotic power devices is called a magnetohydrodynamics engine. This depends on the interaction between magnetic fields and a moving mass, either of fuel or other material that can be affected by electromagnetic fields. This technology has been proposed as a way of making ultraquiet submarines that don't have the noisy propellers that forcibly push their way through water. It also has certain energy-efficiency and pollution-control aspects that make it a candidate for specialized applications, although its expense limits its usefulness today.

Military aviation has also led to the development of radically new jet engines—scramjets and other engines that not only provide rapid propulsion, but also are capable of operating in the thin air of the upper atmosphere. A national transonic transport, or NTT, is under consideration by the U.S. Defense Department and the National Aeronautics and Space Administration for use in both commercial and military applications. The plane, colloquially known as the Tokyo Express, would be able to launch (or take off—no one is sure what the right verb is) from a U.S. airport, pass through the Earth's upper atmosphere like a rocket, and then plunge down toward Tokyo on the other side of the Pacific, reaching its destination in a breathtaking three hours.

NEW POWER TECHNOLOGY

The new U.S. Clean Air Act, passed by Congress in November 1990, mandates the development of alternative fueled automobiles—meaning alternatives to gasoline and diesel fuel. Several regions of the country, including California and the northeastern states, have supplemented this law with programs to speed the development of such automobiles in order to cut air pollution. One of the clearly identified targets of these programs is the electric car. Conceivably, such a car would be plugged into an outlet at night, when electrical demand is low, driven during the day, and then brought back to its recharge site in the evening. Long trips could be accomplished by having removable batteries that store electrical energy; a driver would pull up to a fuel station and switch batteries, just as one might tank up at a fuel pump today.

Such a technology calls for new types of motor designs, although according to most industry researchers, the stumbling block is not the motor, but rather the battery, which tends to be inordinately heavy and not sufficiently powerful for common types of driving today. Thus, like biotechnology, microelectronics, and many other high tech industries, new transportation systems depend on the development of new materials. For the NTT, to cite another example, a big technical obstacle is the need for a jet engine that can burn fuel at extremely high temperatures without disintegrating. Researchers have looked at ceramic-metal composites and new alloys as part of the solution.

POWER TECHNOLOGY FOR SPACE EXPLORATION

In the early 1990s, space exploration has slowed dramatically. The world's two leading pioneers, the United States and the former Soviet

Union, have both scaled back their space programs. In the U.S., problems with technical glitches and massive budgets have plagued the space shuttle program and made the plans for an eventual space station problematic. In the former Soviet Union, the problem is one of generalized economic paralysis—the mighty social and economic monolith that had been the Soviet Union is breaking apart, and pressing economic issues are restricting the large budgets that had supported prestigious space launches.

However, it is doubtful that these obstacles will remain in the way of space exploration for decade after decade. Space dreamers are accustomed to taking a long perspective on their chosen field, and what might not happen in 1997 could happen in 2007 or 2017—still well within the working careers of many high school students today. Space exploration depends on many other things besides new rockets and propulsion systems, but the development of such technologies could provide added momentum to the aspirations of today's space planners. In particular, a more powerful engine could make the trip to Mars appreciably shorter than currently thought. Rocket and engine types barely dreamed about today could change the entire picture of exploring our solar system during the twenty-first century.

Part Three
Preparing for
High Tech Careers

WHAT IS A HIGH TECH RESEARCHER?

"America's Hot Young Scientists" blared the cover of *Fortune* magazine recently. Why a magazine that normally covers the comings and goings of bankers and business managers would put a scientist on its cover is not hard to decipher: "These men and women give the U.S. an edge in the race for global advantage," the article says.

Both in the United States and in Canada, the importance of science and technology to economic growth is now widely recognized. Universities like the Massachusetts Institute of Technology or McGill University are held as national treasures. And while the typical person relates science and high technology to such common goods as videocassette recorders or personal computers, business managers and government officials recognize that the fountainhead of these technologies is research by scientists and engineers with no commercial purpose in mind— "pure" research in mathematics, astronomy, physics, biology, and the other sciences.

The previous section provided a survey of the industries and research organizations that deliver new technologies to the marketplace or to the laboratory. This section will examine the fields of academic study that prepare the student for entering those high tech organizations.

High technology, as previously stated, is dominated by science and engineering graduates. The leading edge of technology—R&D—is often carried out by Ph.D. scientists and engineers. The workers who apply high technology, by installing a computer system in an office or designing a new pollution-control system, for example, usually have a bachelor's or, sometimes, a master's degree. There are many exceptions to these rules of thumb; one prominent exception is that often a liberal arts graduate, or even a high school graduate, can participate in high technology development.

In this section, we'll look at the major groupings of scientific, engineering, and technological college majors that can open the door to a high tech career. We'll also look at the nontechnical programs that produce important secondary professions among high tech organizations. Keep in mind that the high tech field is multidisciplinary. More and more, the academic disciplines that one can study as an undergraduate are leaving major gaps in the knowledge needed to solve new types of problems. It is only when experts from a variety of disciplines gather and pool their collective knowledge that solutions appear. For the individual scientist or engineer, this multidisciplinary need makes it desirable to study in a variety of programs while a student or to explore such options as the double major or the combination of one type of undergraduate degree with a master's degree or Ph.D. in another field. Keep an open mind about the exact major you want to undertake in college and the options you have along the way to graduation.

It is worthwhile to pause a moment before jumping into descriptions of all the professions and academic disciplines that will be described in the following pages to consider scientific R&D in general terms. There are many common elements to high tech work that nearly all of its participants share.

One of the key fundamental aspects of scientific endeavors is that new knowledge of how the world works is drawn from the evidence that researchers gather. In some cases, this evidence is derived from experiments; in others, from observations of the natural world. The first of these is called inductive reasoning, meaning, in a simplified way, that you can generalize about how something works in one test to how the same phenomenon functions throughout the known universe. Electricity coursing through a light bulb in Kansas will cause the same illumination as it would in China.

The second form of research requires the scientist or engineer to make deductions from evidence found where it is observable. Police detectives use the same reasoning: gathering evidence, making assumptions about what that evidence proves, and then looking for more information that will confirm those assumptions. If wheat in Iowa is dying from a mysterious ailment that causes its leaves to turn black, and it is found that a new infectious organism has been discovered in Alberta that causes wheat leaves to blacken, it is not unreasonable to assume that the same organism is infecting Iowa wheat and then to perform tests to isolate it.

Both these forms of research require patient, careful analysis of the observations made during testing or surveying in the field. Careful notes are taken, and this record is reviewed over and over to discover answers. This is the main reason that much scientific progress occurs when a new type of analytical instrument is developed. With the instrument, scientists are able to make observations of things that were unknown previously. It is as if a blind person is now suddenly able to see and can make comparisons between what was only felt in the past and what can now be seen.

Another common aspect of R&D today is that it is collaborative, meaning that many different researchers share in the advances that go on in a field. Sometimes this collaboration is performed actively, with researchers sharing data and coordinating each other's efforts. More often, it is accomplished by the pooling of knowledge that occurs when scientists write papers or give lectures. The number of scientific journals has literally exploded in recent decades, with hundreds of new publications, in many languages, devoted to increasingly specialized areas of science. One of the challenges of modern research is simply to keep up with this flood of information. More than once, it has occurred that a discovery made by one researcher was already common knowledge to another; the two were simply reading different scientific journals.

A third aspect of R&D today is that it is increasingly being sponsored by private industry. This is true throughout much of the industrialized world, both in North America and abroad. One of the differences of private research from any other type is that sometimes the researcher doesn't want to share the information with other researchers. The usual reason is that the industrial sponsor of that research wants to profit from it by using the new knowledge to make a saleable product.

Even when research is carried out among college professors, there are occasions when some of the results are kept from the public because of industrial sponsorship. Weighing against this trend is the rising cost and difficulty of making truly useful, truly revolutionary research happen. Not only are various industrial manufacturers sharing in the cost of research, entire nations are, as is happening with many of the satellite launches made in recent years or with the huge atomic particle accelerators that physicists are using. R&D is a competitive feature of modern economies, but there are more and more cases where it makes sense for nations to share the results so that everyone benefits.

BIOLOGICAL SCIENCES

A mighty force flows through the collegiate and professional experiences of many of those who major in biological sciences: medical school and a career as a medical doctor. There are about 600,000 medical doctors in North America, and many thousands more dentists, therapists, and other healthcare providers. Moreover, the field is expected to be one of the fastest-growing ones among all professions.

A major in one of the biological sciences is not a prerequisite for medical school admission, but many students take it as the closest undergraduate degree to what medical schools teach. And because the competition to get into medical school is intense, these students tend to be the most aggressive in pursuing high scores, both in the classroom and on aptitude and admissions tests.

Medicine, by itself, can certainly be considered a high tech profession; in fact, many people criticize the profession for the overuse of technology in healing the sick. However, there are many other high tech careers for biological sciences majors, particularly in the evolving field of biotechnology.

THE ROOTS OF MEDICINE AND BIOLOGY

While medicine and biology are among the oldest professions and fields of study, it was only in the past two centuries that their study became formalized in collegiate programs. While there were medical schools in Europe after the Renaissance, medical care was as likely to be provided by a midwife or a barber as it was by an academically trained doctor. Medicine has a very colorful, dramatic history, with abrupt changes in the field occurring as new science was developed.

A good example of this is the famed germ theory of disease that evolved during the nineteenth century. As a result of the development of the microscope (in the century before), scientists were able to study bacteria and other microorganisms in a way never possible before. The work of Louis Pasteur (from whose name the "pasteurization" of milk is derived) and others showed that these microbes were the cause of many infectious diseases. Previously, people thought that vapors arising from unhealthful, low-lying regions (which tended to have swampy lands) were the cause. Armed with new understanding, public health officials learned to get pure water or to have existing water boiled and to minimize the contamination of foodstuffs. Epidemics of cholera, malaria, and other fevers faded from the scene.

During the 1800s, too, Charles Darwin made his revolutionary theories about evolution and genetics known by publishing *The Origin of Species,* which attempted to account for the development of new life forms (including humans) over the eons. The understanding of natural selection (which is as much a philosophical statement as a scientific one) as the cause of the wondrous proliferation of life throughout the planet has led to dramatic improvements in understanding how livestock or plants can be upgraded to provide healthier crops and better nutrition for humans. At the same time, Darwin's identification of genetics as the key factor in defining a species set the stage for the research that culminated in the 1950s with the deciphering of DNA as the basic genetic code. This Nobel Prize-winning effort by James Watson and Francis Crick in turn opened up the vista of genetic engineering—the manipulation of DNA and the very definition of living organisms. Modern society and the healthcare system are still reacting to these dramatic discoveries.

If one goes far enough back into the history of medicine and biology, one finds that it was only in recent centuries that they became sciences. To the ancients, health and the fate of one's children were bound up in moral, religious, and philosophical codes of belief. "The sins of the father are passed on to the next generation" is one example, from the Bible, of how medicine and biology were understood. Another factor was, plainly and simply, the inability of doctors to improve the health of their patients. Many sick people of previous centuries lived or were cured despite the efforts of doctors, rather than because of them.

MODERN MEDICAL AND BIOLOGICAL ADVANCES

In the modern era, vast improvements in scientific instruments, such as the microscope, and improved knowledge of chemistry, physics, and mathematics have built a strong scientific basis to biology and medicine. There are new specialties evolving in the field, such as molecular biology, which accept that the principles of living organisms can be explained on the basis of chemical interactions. To be sure, there has also been a growth in scientific knowledge in anthropology, sociology, psychology, psychiatry, and other forms of social science that address the needs of humans and other life forms from a different perspective than chemical interactions. These social sciences give us a better understanding of how individuals interact with each other, but they have less to say about what goes on inside an individual member of a species.

So the high tech, hard science trend in biological sciences continues to intensify. In the 1980s, scientists began experimenting with changing the chemicals that make up the DNA code of life and were able to change them and see the effects of these changes in living creatures. One result of these genetic manipulations has been the creation of very sophisticated diagnostic tools that enable doctors, for example, to tell us what is going on inside our bodies without cutting them open. Another result has been the effort to cure humans (and many animals) of genetic disorders such as cancer that have been the scourge of humanity for ages.

WHAT BIOLOGISTS DO

Biologists work in laboratories, conducting experiments in which cells are broken apart and the bits of genetic material are collected and then analyzed. Over the years, methods have been established to alter this genetic material—to splice genes from one species into the DNA of another. The product of this gene splicing can then be reinserted back into another living cell, and as that cell reproduces and divides, organisms are created that have a new genetic makeup. Once enough of the cells have been grown, they can be collected in a vessel and manipulated to produce desired biochemicals.

For most research applications, a doctorate degree is highly desirable. The laboratory work is similar to what goes on in college laboratories or even, in a much more sophisticated way, high school laboratories. The main differences, aside from the greater complexity of college-level work, are the access to expensive, sophisticated analytical instruments and the greater use of computers to arrange and then analyze experimental results. Biological research doesn't go on only in the laboratory; many scientists spend most of their time in the field, collecting samples of life forms and studying the patterns of living systems in different environments. In addition, there is a tremendous network—the largest of any of the sciences—in laboratories and research stations sponsored by hospitals, pharmaceutical companies, government, academic institutions, and private research facilities. It is quite common for a philanthropist to have funded the development of a facility to study a particular disease or physical ailment.

Once a set of experiments has been performed and new results successfully obtained, the scientist may publish an article or give a lecture on the subject announcing the findings. At the same time, patent lawyers may be contacted to protect the technology by obtaining patents from government organizations such as the U.S. Patent Office. Sometimes the researcher will follow a new technical development out of the laboratory and into the management of a pharmaceutical company or hospital where the innovation is put to practical use. Many medical researchers run clinics in conjunction with their research laboratories in order to test new results and to formulate appropriate procedures for using an innovation. In the United States, the Food and Drug Administration (FDA) plays a central role in this process. In the U.S., unlike many other countries, not only does a new medication or medical procedure have to be harmless to those who need it. The innovation must also work as advertised—that is, it must have a beneficial effect on patients.

To demonstrate the lack of harm and the positive benefits of a medical discovery, those who would commercialize that technology must pass a rigorous series of trials and test runs that are approved by the FDA. These validation tests are a complex and expensive undertaking in and of themselves. Very often, an organization like a pharmaceutical company will have one group of researchers who develop new medications and another who perform the validation tests. A heavy involvement in statistical analyses is part of the validation process.

WHAT BIOLOGY STUDENTS STUDY

Much of biological education is the assimilation of large numbers of facts. Students study basic chemistry and introductory biology, which familiarizes them with the processes of biological research. Then a broad variety of specialized courses can be taken that reflect the great number of disciplines under the biology banner. Along the way, the student learns details of the wondrous variety of life, from the biochemicals that make it up to the many organs and systems of life forms to the variety of species of plant and animal life.

In upper-level classes, and especially in graduate school, the many subdisciplines under biology become apparent. Practically every life form has a body of knowledge associated with it, which the student can choose to study. Here is a partial list:

Biochemistry—the study of the chemical basis of life.
Molecular biology—the study of the structure and function of biochemicals and genetic matter in cells.
Physiology—the study of the structural composition of life forms.
Genetics—the study of reproduction and inherited traits.
Ecology—the study of the interactions of living things with each other and with the environment.

It is also possible to specialize in distinct families of living things: entomology (insects); ornithology (birds); botany (plants); zoology (all animals); ichthyology (fish); paleontology (extinct, fossilized life forms); herpetology (reptiles); primatology (apes and other human-like animals); and others. Mention of entomology, to take one example, might strike one at first as a rather boring process of chasing butterflies across the fields. But to demonstrate how high technology intrudes even here, consider that chemical companies seeking to develop new pesticides depend on entomologists to reveal how insect species survive and how they might be controlled. Entomology has also become important in many environmental applications, especially where rare species are threatened by human encroachment.

With this diverse array of specialties, it's no wonder that over 25 percent of biologists go on to graduate school, in addition to the thousands who head for the nation's medical schools. A great distinction is made among medical researchers between those who perform clinical work, meaning that they deal regularly with patients, and those who do not. There are plenty of doctoral-level researchers, working on illnesses or injuries of humans, who practically never work with an actual patient. Rather, they work on samples of cells, or even on a few vials of some biochemical drawn from tissues of human patients or from organisms (such as bacteria or viruses) that infect humans.

Biological high tech work is not reserved only for the doctoral-level graduate, of course. Important developmental work is done in industrial production of foods and medicines by those with bachelor's degrees. In addition, there are many positions to be filled in the regulation of medical and food-production technologies, which is usually carried out by government-employed inspectors. Finally, there are numerous positions at laboratories—in hospitals or clinics, pharmaceutical companies, food producers, and at colleges or privately sponsored research organizations—where tests and diagnostic procedures are carried out. This work is very demanding, but also very specialized, featuring a technician who concentrates on the operation of one type of instrument or one type of test. As with research work generally, this work requires careful, patient evaluation of test procedures and results.

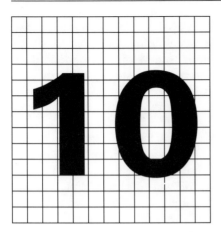

CHEMICAL ENGINEERING

Chemical engineering is one of the smaller, more specialized engineering disciplines, but one that has attracted a substantial number of graduates in recent years. The largest number of chemical engineering graduates are employed by the chemical industry, but the nature of the chemical engineering education also makes its graduates attractive to a broad variety of employers, including aerospace and automotive firms, electronics manufacturers, oil and mineral producers, and agriculture and forestry products companies. There are about 50,000 practicing chemical engineers in the United States, according to data from the Bureau of Labor Statistics, and almost 6,000 Canadian chemical engineers, according to Canadian Census data.

If you think of engineering generally as the application of scientific principles to manufacturing or construction problems, then chemical engineering is the application of the principles of chemistry to those same problems. Where a chemist makes a discovery by creating a reaction that combines one raw material with another for some third chemical, the chemical engineer reaches a goal when that reaction can be carried out in tonnage quantities, using vessels that contain thousands of gallons, at a large, modern chemical manufacturing facility.

THE ROOTS OF CHEMICAL ENGINEERING

Chemical engineering arose late in the last century as the chemical industry itself became an international power in North America. This industry was greatly enlarged by the vast quantities of minerals and forestry products (paper and chemicals derived from wood) that the expansion in the western regions of North America created. Manufacturers that had been accustomed to producing materials in small quantities were now faced with much greater demand for these materials, so they sought ways to improve the efficiency of chemical manufacturing technology.

A key concept that arose in the teaching of chemical engineering early in this century is that of the unit operation. Unit operations are a way of rigorously defining such common chemical manufacturing steps as evaporation, distillation, mixing, refining, and reacting. A variety of mathematical descriptions were written about each unit operation, and the equipment and procedures required to improve the efficiency of that operation were then devised. In Europe, on the other hand, the model of chemical manufacturing still very much followed the principles of a chemistry laboratory, but "scaled up" (as the term is used in the business) to a very large size.

In the 1920s, developments in North American chemical engineering helped increase the supply of petroleum-based fuels for the booming automobile business. In the 1930s, many of the original plastics and polymeric materials that are so common today were commercialized: nylon, polyethylene and polypropylene (used in packaging), polyvinyl chloride (used in plastic pipes), and others. Chlorofluorocarbons, the chemicals now of great concern because of their damage to the ozone layer of the atmosphere, originated at this time as a miraculously helpful compound that replaced toxic or flammable materials in domestic refrigerators.

In the 1940s, chemical engineers helped devise ways to mass-produce penicillin (the newly developed antibiotic that saved the lives of so many wounded soldiers) and synthetic rubber (to replace supplies of natural rubber cut off from the Far East). Late in World War II, chemical engineering expertise was essential in helping to produce sufficient quantities of radioactive materials for the first atomic weapons, which were used in Japan in 1945 to bring the war to an end.

In the 1950s and 1960s, North American economies boomed as a consumer-oriented society was created. Vast new quantities of construction materials were required—from plastics for packaging and consumer goods to fuels for the automotive and airline industries. The 1950s are remembered now as the time when synthetics took hold in the minds of consumers as the latest, best products; later, as the environmental problems of chemical production became clearer, synthetic became a synonym for shoddy merchandise—although the quantity of synthetics produced has hardly declined.

CHEMICAL ENGINEERING AND THE ENVIRONMENT

Environmental problems have been closely associated with the chemical industry since the 1960s. Many observers date the connection to the publication in 1962 of *Silent Spring* by the marine biologist Rachel Carson, who brought national attention to the realization that widespread use of petrochemical-based pesticides (especially the compound known as DDT) was destroying wildlife. In defense of chemical engineering, it can truly be said that chemical engineers were producing materials that society wanted at the time, according to standards that were acceptable at the time. However, those products and standards have left a legacy of pollution and environmental damage that the entire world is contending with today.

Chemical engineering has undergone something of a revolution in recent years as the seriousness of the environmental issues confronting society has become clear. Today, in fact, chemical engineering is playing an instrumental role in cleaning up past pollution and in preventing further environmental damage. Acid rain—an issue of concern to both the United States and Canada—is minimized when utilities or factories that burn coal or other sulfur-laden materials control the output of sulfur by-products. But to do this, a chemical reactor called a scrubber must be used after the combustion process. The scrubber neutralizes the sulfur compounds, and in some cases allows them to be drawn out as pure sulfur, which is itself a valuable industrial commodity.

WHAT CHEMICAL ENGINEERS DO

At the outset of the 1990s, the prospects are excellent for good employment in chemical engineering. Ironically, this is because the number of students pursuing a chemical engineering degree has fallen so much. When enrollments in chemical engineering peaked in the mid-1980s, there were nearly 8,000 degrees being awarded in the U.S. each year. Now, at the bachelor's level, the number is below 4,000 (below 600 in Canada). Yet industry's demand for chemical engineers has been rising. Employment prospects in environmental work are especially promising.

The job functions that working chemical engineers fulfill depend on the type of organization at which they are employed. Typically in manufacturing organizations, chemical engineers are production managers or process engineers. A production engineer works to keep the facility running as it was designed to and oversees the efforts of the production staff. Process engineers do not have everyday responsibility, but rather work to improve the efficiency, safety, or productivity of a plant by redesigning components or by changing production practices.

Many chemical engineers are employed at engineering/design firms, where they provide design and construction expertise needed when a client company desires a new chemical plant to be built. Most chemical companies no longer manage their own construction projects; rather, they call in an engineering/design firm. After the preliminary design goals are set between the designer and the client, staffs of engineers specify the various types of equipment needed, lay out the design for the pipes and electrical connections, and write the initial operating procedures. Starting up a chemical plant is not a simple matter of turning a switch; a complicated, multi-step process is undertaken, and it must be done in the proper order. Once the plant is running, its operation reverts to the production engineers.

Both chemical companies and engineering/design firms employ chemical engineers to develop new chemical products or production methods. This developmental engineering work requires close coordination with chemists and other researchers. A key tool for the developmental engineer is the pilot plant, which is a reduced-scale version of an actual production facility. Pilot plants can be complex, multi-million-dollar facilities all by themselves. The goal is to provide data on how a full-scale facility should be run. The pilot plant is where the developmental engineers perform much of their experimentation.

WHAT CHEMICAL ENGINEERING STUDENTS STUDY

Like other engineers, chemical engineering students begin their education with basic chemistry, physics, and mathematics courses. The mathematics extends through the sophomore year, including advanced calculus, linear algebra, and differential equations. The chemistry continues beyond the introductory courses to organic chemistry, physical chemistry, and possibly biochemistry or biology. Biology courses are important for chemical engineers who intend to pursue a career in the pharmaceutical or food industries.

Chemical engineering courses include the fundamentals of unit operations, thermodynamics and fluid mechanics, and a design course with a title like "project engineering." In this course, the student attempts to draw together principles of good engineering design with principles of economics, resulting in a manufacturing plant that runs profitably. The options that chemical engineering students can pursue include courses in metallurgy or materials engineering, computer science, electronics manufacturing, biotechnology, or environmental engineering design.

At the graduate level, students concentrate on an area of importance to a particular industry or pursue a research direction that will ultimately lead to a new understanding of some basic body of knowledge about chemical engineering. Fluid dynamics—the properties of fluids as they pass through pipes, into reactors, or through distillation or separation devices—is one such basic area. When the student seeks employment in a particular industry, courses in such topics as petroleum refining, pulp and paper production, pharmaceuticals, microelectronics, metallurgy, and others can be pursued.

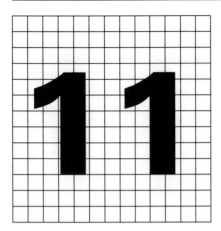

CHEMISTRY

Chemistry is one of the basic sciences. It tells us much about how the natural world works, and it guides researchers to determine what products can be manufactured. While many specialized industries, such as electronics, metallurgy, ceramics, foods, and pharmaceuticals, have their own technologies and manufacturing methods, all of them depend on chemistry and chemists to provide the fundamental knowledge necessary to design and make products.

Even so, relatively few chemists are involved in actual production—this is usually left to engineering staffs. Rather, the working chemist helps design new products and production methods and maintains checks on the quality of goods that are produced. Nearly every manufacturer has a staff of quality control chemists who monitor factory output; these chemists continually review product quality by running standardized tests for purity, strength, and other criteria.

THE ROOTS OF CHEMISTRY

In ancient times, chemistry was a popular filter through which to philosophize about nature and the universe, but many of the theories about those topics were clouded in mystical beliefs. An example of this was the theory by ancient Greeks and others that all matter was composed of various proportions of earth, water, air, and fire. Still, the ancients were able to develop metals, glass, and ceramics, so the theorizing had some practical effect.

In the Middle Ages, what chemical research and teaching there was existed primarily among alchemists. Alchemy is usually associated with magic and mysticism, not science, but in its time, some of the most prominent researchers of their era were alchemists. Isaac Newton, the scientist who helped define modern physics, is one example. Alchemists strove to create gold from base matter and to find a compound that would provide eternal life. While neither of these goals was achieved (although modern nuclear physics now makes it possible to create gold from something else), alchemists developed many procedures for conducting research, processing materials, and measuring the effects of chemical reactions.

"Modern" chemistry began to take shape in Europe in the 1700s, as such scientists as the Frenchman Antoine Lavoisier and the Englishman John Dalton developed sound theories about the atomic nature of matter and elementary chemical reactions. In the 1800s, the periodic table of the elements was established, and scientists around the world raced to fill out the lists of chemical categories that the periodic table predicted. Also during the 1800s, German and English textile manufacturers established programs of developing dyes and textile-treating chemicals; this led to the formalized structure of organic chemistry (the chemistry of carbon compounds). By now, academic programs at leading universities in both the Old and New Worlds were established.

Organic chemicals—initially from coal, later from petroleum—became the driving force of much chemical research in the early 1900s. The first plastics were commercialized, and much of the underlying theory of chemical reactions and structure was established. During the same period, a combination of chemistry and physics research established nuclear physics and began exploring subatomic matter.

In the 1920s and 1930s, chemists and chemical engineers paced each other in developing new materials and new ways of manufacturing them. Thus began the reign of synthetics, such as plastics, textiles, and construction materials, that were thought to be better products because they were human-made. Out of the laboratories and factories came nylon, polyethylene, synthetic rubber, latex paints, high-octane gasoline, pesticides, artificial vitamins, food preservatives, and a veritable cornucopia of other products. World War II spurred this growth and also led to the development of atomic power. In the 1950s, the rise of the consumer society added momentum to these developments. The invention of the transistor in the early 1950s demonstrated the importance of chemistry in the nascent electronics industry.

During this period, too, a pattern emerged of chemical research sponsored by industrial corporations. DuPont, the large chemical and energy firm, set the pace with an industrial laboratory led by Wallace Carothers, a Harvard chemist. The pattern was to set up a modern laboratory, staff it with doctoral-level chemists, and guide the progress of applied (meaning, capable of being commercialized) research. Oil, agricultural, and metals companies followed suit.

In the 1960s, a backlash began to develop to the rise of synthetic chemicals. The turning point was the 1962 book *Silent Spring* by the marine biologist Rachel Carson. Carson warned against the practice of indiscriminate spraying of pesticides across the countryside, which killed not only their target—mosquitoes and other pests—but also birds, beneficial insects, and other wildlife. Her book ultimately led to a ban on DDT, a common pesticide.

MODERN CHEMISTRY

Chemistry had grown to a rich and diverse field by the 1960s. As chemical knowledge forged ahead in various sectors of manufacturing and agriculture, new fundamental research by chemists opened up yet other fields for chemists' employment, including such areas as analytical chemistry and biochemistry. Here is a generalized grouping of today's chemistry subdisciplines.

Agricultural chemistry—the study of fertilizers, pesticides, and soil chemistry.

Analytical chemistry—the study of how to develop instruments and ways to measure chemical properties.

Biochemistry—the study of the chemical nature of life.

Environmental chemistry—the study of the interaction of synthetic chemicals in the environment.

Food science—the study of how to improve or alter foodstuffs to develop healthier foods, such as low-fat foods.

Geochemistry—the study of the chemical processes in the Earth.

Materials science—the study of the development of new, commercially useful materials.

Organic chemistry—the study of chemicals based on carbon.

Physical chemistry—the study of the atomic and bulk properties of chemicals.

Radiochemistry—the study of the effects of radiation and radioactivity on chemicals (sometimes this is called **nuclear chemistry**).

With such a plethora of specializations, it makes sense for many students to go on to graduate school simply to acquire the knowledge necessary to practice effectively in one of these specialties.

WHAT CHEMISTS DO

According to data from the American Chemical Society (ACS), there were about 9,000 chemistry students with BS or BA degrees graduating annually in the late 1980s. Enrollments have been declining for several years. About 20 percent of undergraduate chemists go on to graduate school, and most of those continue until a doctorate degree is earned.

Also according to ACS, just over half of all chemists work in manufacturing; 19 percent work in teaching and research; about 15 percent work in nonmanufacturing businesses; and the remainder work in government.

In industry, chemists function in certain production roles, but are more often involved in quality control, testing, and process engineering. Many chemists, especially those with advanced degrees, perform R&D in the laboratories that manufacturers operate. In government, chemists conduct research and also are called on for regulatory inspections of the safety of manufactured products and the environmental quality of manufacturing processes.

A perfect example of the energy and excitement in chemistry today can be seen by the race to understand the carbon crystal called buckminsterfullerene (more popularly, buckyballs). Buckminsterfullerene is named after the 1960s architect Buckminster Fuller, who popularized the geodesic dome as an inexpensive but efficient way to build shelter. The chemical buckyball is a hollow, sphere-like crystal of interconnected carbon atoms. The first experiments simply confirmed its existence as a stable chemical structure. Later experiments showed that what was thought to be a rare, expensive-to-produce material was in fact almost as common as dirt and could be made cheaply. Now, in the latest twist, chemists have seen indications that buckyballs could be superconducting—capable of carrying an electrical current at relatively high temperatures.

What is to be done with this intriguing substance? Early on, researchers theorized that a fluid containing a large amount of buckminsterfullerene might be an excellent lubricant, with all the little spheres acting as smooth-rolling ball bearings. Other chemists have experimented with encapsulating a metal atom inside the interior space of the crystal. Still others are looking at how to manufacture the material cheaply. Each passing month brings new information to light about this wonderful substance.

Chemistry is a great gateway college discipline in the sense that undergraduates with this degree are able to venture broadly in professional schooling and careers. Chemistry is a great preparation for medical school. Some chemists combine this technical knowledge with the study of law or public policy; others expand their technical expertise by studying engineering or another science.

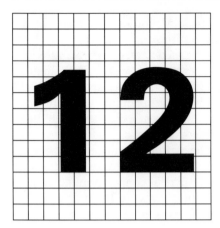

CIVIL ENGINEERING

Civil engineering has the richest history and tradition of any of the engineering disciplines. It was practiced in ancient times, became more advanced during the Middle Ages, and grew dramatically during the nineteenth and twentieth centuries. It is a large profession and is the one usually thought of when the word "engineer" is mentioned.

Unfortunately, this tradition has also served to limit civil engineering's perspective on the future. In the United States, and in much of the rest of the world, relatively little R&D has been performed on construction technology and other areas of employment for civil engineers. Many of the large construction firms that build the skyscrapers and highways around the continent do their work pretty much the way they did twenty-five or even fifty years ago. There are, of course, innovations in construction machinery and techniques occurring all the time, but they tend to be small steps rather than great leaps.

There are also good reasons for this conservatism. Innovations like new computer chips or mechanical devices can be tried out on a small scale, and if they don't work, the component can be replaced or junked with little loss. To build a bridge or skyscraper with an innovative technology that doesn't work, however, is to cause a horrendously expensive problem that could bankrupt the construction company, the building owner, and others and give the entire construction industry a black eye. There are strict safety codes written for most types of construction that often specify not only what materials should be used to build something, but how the work should proceed. Changes are made only slowly.

There are signs of a new attitude, however. Many construction experts see that dramatic innovations are occurring overseas. In Japan, for example, "smart" skyscrapers are being constructed that have internal mechanisms for adjusting to earthquake shocks without damaging the building. Japan is also the source of much new technology in prefabricated housing, in which homes can be built in modules in a factory, shipped to a site, and hooked together in a matter of days. Wisely applied, such technology could do much to reduce the cost of housing and cure some of the problems of homelessness that burden the larger cities in North America.

Concerned about the lack of technological R&D, governmental organizations like the National Science Foundation and some universities have organized R&D programs. The construction industry is also stepping up its support of R&D.

Meanwhile, there is a considerable effort going on to change how civil engineers do their design work before construction starts. In particular, computer-aided design (CAD) programs that help scope out a project are now a common feature in engineering design offices. CAD programs help speed up the design process by eliminating much of the tedious drafting and error-correcting that goes on during the design phase. CAD programs are also helping engineers develop designs that are pre-tested (in the computer) for their strength and reliability. A civil engineer with a new idea for designing some building component can draw it in a CAD program and then run another program that analyzes the stresses and weights on the component.

OTHER CIVIL ENGINEERING PROFESSIONS

Civil engineering is not totally composed of builders. A large portion of the civil engineering profession is devoted to resolving problems with municipal water supplies, land development or preservation, waste disposal, and environmental remediation. On many college campuses, the civil engineering department is now the department of civil and environmental engineering, and many students interested solely in environmental engineering topics join the civil engineering department.

One of the more intriguing trends occurring in land development today is the attempt to restore parklands or wildlife refuges to their natural state through the use of engineering and biological sciences. In an earlier era, civil engineers were praised for draining disease-causing swamplands; now and in the future, society is calling on the profession to help build and preserve swamps as a way of conserving rare plant and animal species.

Another significant portion of the civil engineering workforce is employed by the manufacturers of construction materials—lumber, stone, brick and ceramics, heating and cooling systems, and paints and coatings. In this area, the civil engineer is a materials scientist, helping to design and test new materials. Technological advancements are occurring rapidly in the material sciences, a trend that affects many other science and engineering professions.

A good example of how new technology will influence future materials technology is being showcased near Pittsfield, Massachusetts, where General Electric has built a home of the future. The futuristic-looking house features such innovations as windows whose tinting can be adjusted to sunlight conditions (eliminating the need for window coverings) and heating and ventilation components that can be plugged in or unplugged almost like appliances, thus making changes or servicing much easier. Most intriguingly, the building is designed to make use of structural materials that have been recycled from industrial municipal garbage, such as plastics and ceramics. If only a small portion of the materials the construction industry uses could be diverted from the waste stream, a great relief on overburdened disposal systems could be achieved.

WHAT CIVIL ENGINEERING STUDENTS STUDY

The education of civil engineers begins with the introductory math, physics, and chemistry courses that all engineering students usually take. These are followed by courses in surveying and mapping, structural mechanics, and materials science. Design courses, using the skills learned in mechanics and materials science, are then offered. Optional programs in natural resources development, soil science, hydraulics, and highway construction finish off the undergraduate education.

Because a great number of working civil engineers are employed at small design and construction companies, civil engineers tend to stress business management skills, both in their education and after college. Compared to other engineering disciplines, a much higher proportion of civil engineers obtain a professional engineering license. This license, offered by state governments, permits the holder to work on public works projects; many clients of engineering companies also insist on having licensed engineers complete their projects.

At the graduate level, many civil engineers intensify their knowledge of particular construction technologies. They can also specialize in environmental issues, transportation, forestry or mining, and ocean or coastal engineering. Because of the close interaction between civil engineering and public government, many graduate students choose to study public administration, public policy and other governmental topics. Civil engineers with this background can then take roles in government administration.

The number of new civil engineers has been steadily declining in the United States in recent years, having gone from almost 10,000 bachelor's degree graduates per year in the early 1980s to about 7,500 at the end of the decade. In Canada, the numbers have held at about 1,000 per year.

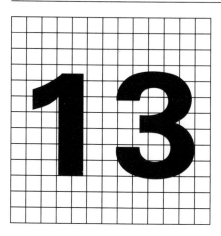

COMPUTER SCIENCE
AND ENGINEERING

Who hasn't seen the movie *2001: A Space Odyssey*? In that film, an immensely powerful computer named HAL took over the control of a space ship, killing most of its crew and creating a frightening situation for the hero of the movie to solve. That movie said a lot to people of the time about computers: that they were big and powerful, inhuman, and not to be trusted.

Fast forward to the 1980s, when a spate of movies appeared featuring robots that liked people, were small and cuddly, and acted more or less like a faithful dog to their human owners. Some robots, like the Terminator that Arnold Schwartzeneggar brought to life, started out as bad guys but later became good guys.

What has changed during the intervening years? Simply put, we have learned to accept computers rather than be afraid of them. The advent of the personal computer (PC), invented in the late 1970s, has played a major role in this transformation. Most schools today have PCs that help students learn reading and mathematics and that can be programmed by the student to run all sorts of games and other fun activities. It's a long way from the ominous HAL.

This evolution of computers says a lot about where computers fit into society today. Computers are a common feature of offices, schools, and many homes. They are being used for a great variety of purposes. By the same token, the people who work in computer science and engineering find that they must be familiar not only with scientific programs or massive data files (known as databases), but also games, instructional methods, library science, and other less technical subjects.

As with electrical engineering, even though the past twenty years have seen dramatic changes in computer programming, even more dramatic changes are ahead. As the size and cost of computers shrinks, their usefulness becomes apparent to more and more people. Meanwhile, at the front end of computer research, where unbelievably powerful machines are being designed and built, there is an expectation that they will help solve seemingly impossible problems like weather forecasting or economic planning.

WHAT COMPUTER SCIENTISTS AND ENGINEERS DO

If you are good at mathematics and logic, you can be good at computer science and engineering. The profession involves a math-like ability to define functions precisely and to assemble these functions or instructions in an orderly way so that a program can be successfully run on a computer. Both in terms of the teaching of computer science and the work that professional computer scientists perform, there is a need to keep up with advances in electronics as well as the evolution in the theory of computer programming itself. New computer languages appear regularly, and the ability to keep up with these changes is important to a successful career.

A good example of this that became prominent during the 1980s is a technical subject called on-line transaction processing, or OLTP. The most familiar use of this is at banking machines, where a customer inputs a few keystrokes and has access to his or her bank account. Cash can be withdrawn, funds can be transferred electronically from one account to another, or information can be obtained on the status of one's account. Hidden from the customer's view is a large computer with a program that must be able to update the information for the customer very rapidly. At the same time that cash is being withdrawn, the bank may be receiving checks that the customer wrote days ago. All this information must be kept current and must be stored in a way that is absolutely reliable. You don't want to go to the bank one day and be told that your money has been "lost" by the computer and that therefore you are broke.

OLTP is also useful for department stores that want to keep precise track of what goods are being purchased most rapidly, or for the control systems of factories where it is important to know where the inventory is even as new products are being manufactured. As OLTP technology evolved for banking, it also became useful to other types of users.

Although computer science and engineering are being talked about together in this section, they are evolving into two separate fields. Computer engineers generally are concerned with the hardware and software that are integral to a computer—the microcode, as they are called, that is stored inside a computer regardless of what programs are being run. Computer scientists, who are often called systems analysts in the working world, are concerned with the programs that are run on the computer. They can be totally indifferent to what type of computer is running the program as long as the program runs successfully.

Just as computer hardware has advanced, so has computer software programming. In particular, new languages appear that enable the systems analyst to write different types of programs or to run programs more efficiently. In general, the improvements in computer hardware have progressed faster than those in computer software, so the computer industry as a whole now finds itself being slowed down by the difficulties in writing new programs efficiently. For this reason, there is a strong trend toward a field called software engineering that uses computer programs to write other computer programs.

WHAT COMPUTER SCIENCE AND ENGINEERING STUDENTS STUDY

On college campuses, there are generally three types of arrangements among computer science, computer engineering, and the closely related field of electrical engineering. In one case, a school will have three separate departments, with computer science generally part of the arts and sciences division of the school (where chemistry, physics, and other sciences are also taught). Computer engineering will be part of the engineering school. In this setup, computer science is one of the liberal arts; thus the math and science requirements that most engineering students are required to fulfill are absent.

In the second possibility, the computer science department is part of the engineering school, and there will be some accommodation made for students who don't want to be engineers, but do want to study computer science. Many such schools have other programs in what is called information technology that are part of the liberal arts division of the university. Information technology is oriented more to the uses of computers for storing data or controlling communications than to computer design and construction itself.

In the third case, there is only computer science or electrical engineering. Students who want to be computer engineers get a degree in electrical engineering and concentrate their course options on computer-related topics. The computer science wing may or may not be part of the engineering school.

There are subtle variations to each of these cases, so it is important for high school students to research the placement of the computer disciplines at the school they want to attend.

WHAT LIES AHEAD FOR COMPUTER SCIENTISTS AND ENGINEERS

What lies in store for computer science and engineering? Without a doubt, one of the more exciting trends is the development of artificial intelligence (AI) programming. In this newly evolving field, computer programs are written that enable the program to "learn" on the basis of running through the program repeatedly and then analyzing the results obtained. Artificial intelligence has been a popular research topic for decades, but only recently has the technology developed to the point where it is more than a laboratory curiosity. An important element of AI research, whether or not one agrees that computers can "think," is that the programs are written to address situations where a precise instruction cannot be given. The program must allow for some judgmental decision-making to occur.

There were about 37,000 computer science and engineering graduates at the bachelor's level in the late 1980s in the United States. There were about 4,000 computer engineering graduates. In Canada, there were about 400 computer engineers. The job outlook is good, although new graduates need to be selective about what specific field they enter. In general, the major computer manufacturers have been shedding staff, while companies that specialize in computer software have been growing. There is a pronounced trend toward computer consulting services in which a company produces neither its own hardware nor its own software, but rather advises a client on what computer technology it should purchase.

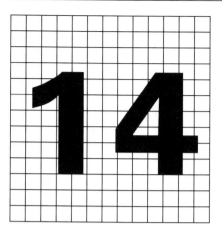

EARTH SCIENCES

The earth sciences include geology, geophysics, atmospheric science, meteorology, and oceanology and oceanography, along with several specialized academic programs. Earth sciences are enjoying a renaissance in the 1990s because of growing worries over the global environment and because of the intensified interest in locating and exploiting natural resources like oil or minerals.

THE ROOTS OF THE EARTH SCIENCES

The earth sciences represent one of humanity's oldest forms of technological development. Prehistoric times are divided among the Stone, Iron, and Bronze Ages on the basis of the ability of the cultures of those eras to extract metals from the ground. Mines have been dug since the beginning of recorded history. As cities came to be organized between 2000 and 1000 B.C., geological skills were developed to obtain and distribute water for agricultural and drinking purposes.

Another great root of the earth sciences was navigation. As the ancient Near Eastern cultures spread along the Mediterranean coasts, the need for predictable voyaging became obvious. Records were kept of ocean currents and wind patterns, and maps were drawn. The nautical skills of the times were bound up in partly philosophical, partly religious beliefs concerning the sun, the stars, and the oceans and land masses.

The missing element in this picture of the ancient knowledge of the earth sciences is meteorology. Because of the weather's tremendous influence over the success of agriculture, most ancient cultures attributed divine powers to the winds and seasons. Unfortunately, there were few ways to research the weather in any sort of quantitative fashion simply because there were no instruments available and the concepts of air pressure, wind movement, and humidity were only vaguely understood.

With the great voyages of the Spanish, Portuguese, and English explorers of the fifteenth and sixteenth centuries, a new world of study opened up for mapmakers, geographers, and mine explorers. Because of the intense concentration of the Spanish on getting gold and other precious metals out of their new empires, the need for better scientific knowledge grew.

The 1800s are looked upon as a golden era of newly created geological knowledge. The existence of fossils, vaguely studied in Europe but with more exciting potential in the New World (where both living and fossilized species unknown to Europe were found), led to new theories about the Earth. Such giants of geology as the Englishman Charles Lyell, the German Alexander von Humboldt, and the Swiss Louis Agassiz created whole new bodies of knowledge about the Earth based in part on their studies of the New World. Charles Darwin, a protegé of Lyell, began his studies on the sailing ship *Beagle* during the 1830s; he soon focused on evolutionary biology as the abundance of new species became known to him during his travels.

Beginning in the Renaissance of the 1300s and 1400s and greatly intensifying during the 1800s, the development of scientific instruments helped to resolve a host of issues relating to the atmosphere and to weather. By the beginning of this century, a host of instruments had been developed that could measure the goings-on in the sky and across the oceans. The use of balloons and early aircraft greatly stepped up the measurements that scientists could make in the atmosphere. During the 1930s, and with much greater impact after the Second World War, the use of rockets and satellites provided earth scientists with vast new concentrations of data to study.

Also in this century, the close association of earth sciences with the petroleum industry began. The chances of finding oil are so daunting, and the expertise that geologists and other earth scientists can provide is so valuable, that industry has paid lavishly for a great variety of studies. These studies have expanded the scientific understanding of the Earth's crust and helped oil producers find new sources of this valuable commodity.

WHAT EARTH SCIENTISTS DO

There are three main trends to the study of the Earth today. One is to understand the weather better and how to predict it. Another is to better understand how to find and exploit buried resources such as oil and minerals. The third is to understand the environmental needs of the world— for pure drinking water, for decontamination of polluted lands, and for understanding the fate of synthetic chemicals in the atmosphere—which is driving the earth sciences in new directions. As a result of the spate of environmental laws that have been passed during the past twenty years, it is easy to say that more is now known about the movement of water and chemicals through the ground than has ever been known before. A fourth theme, not as prominent as the others, is the search for a method to predict earthquakes.

Scientists working on the Earth strive to obtain the very latest instruments to further their efforts. A number of satellites now provide detailed information not only of the trees and highways on the Earth's surface, but also of mineral veins and ocean currents under the surface (this is done through the use of infrared and other forms of light). Armed with this knowledge, scientists and engineers are able to allocate resources for oil and mineral exploration better, to monitor the effects of pollution and urbanization, and to gain a better understanding of how the Earth works.

In the United States, about half of all geoscientists are employed by the oil and natural gas industries. In Canada, the proportion is probably even higher due to the heavy concentration of energy and mineral industries in the west. Of the remaining 50 percent in the United States, about half of those (25 percent of the total) are employed in government—especially the U.S. Geological Survey—and the rest are in consulting. This last category has grown dramatically in recent years due to the vastly increased spending on environmental preservation and remediation.

The needs of the environment draw together many threads of modern geologic and meteorological research today. In the past fifteen years or so, a theory arose that attributed the end of the age of dinosaurs about 65 million years ago to the collision of an asteroid or similar heavenly body with the Earth. The evidence is found in the K-T boundary, the technical term for a fine layer of rock that can be found sandwiched between the rocks that were formed during the years in which dinosaurs lived and the changed environment thereafter. Over the past decade, the evidence has mounted that this is indeed the reason for the mass extinction of dinosaurs—a question that has puzzled scientists and laypeople alike for decades.

What does this have to do with environmental issues? Simply put, it makes people realize that the climate and living conditions of the planet can be changed dramatically—the Earth is not a static, eternal thing, but rather a system that continually adjusts to external conditions. This itself has led to the Gaia hypothesis, a theory (and it is only that) by an English scientist, James Lovelock, that the Earth is alive through the interaction between animate and inanimate matter. Both the K-T boundary question and the Gaia hypothesis are important concepts to keep in mind when considering an issue such as the effects of chlorofluorocarbon molecules on the Earth's upper atmosphere or of global warming caused by the rising concentration of carbon dioxide gas (the end result of combustion) in the atmosphere.

WHAT EARTH SCIENCE STUDENTS STUDY

As the previous examples show, the earth sciences are a lively field today. On college campuses, most earth sciences programs are dominated by the geology department. Students first take courses in the basics of science—chemistry, mathematics, and perhaps physics. Then a series of courses teach the fundamental principles of earth science—the formation and disposition of rocks, the effects of water on the Earth's crust, and the forces that shape continents, mountains, and sea coasts. Students seeking to specialize in meteorology will add courses on the atmosphere; students seeking a career in the oil industry will add courses on petroleum and geological mapping.

Graduates with a B.S. or B.A. degree can find careers in the oil and gas industries, mining, and consulting firms that work on construction or environmental projects. During the early 1980s, the petroleum industry in the United States underwent a tremendous shrinkage as the price of oil, which had skyrocketed during the 1970s, dropped precipitously. This price has changed very little, which constrains the amount of exploration and production that oil companies will undertake. Still, worldwide production of oil is on the rise, and oil companies are among the largest corporations in the world.

If earth science students choose to go on to graduate school, opportunities in research open up. Most meteorological positions require at least a master's degree. The U.S. government sponsors much geological research because of its importance to domestic industries. And, of course, doctoral-level earth scientists can teach, a field that is expected to grow because of the increased number of students and experienced professionals who seek to perform environmental work.

There were about 7,000 degrees awarded in the U.S. in the earth sciences each year in the late 1980s; of these, about 500 were for Ph.D. graduates.

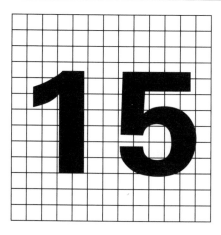

ELECTRICAL ENGINEERING

Electrical engineering is the giant among engineering professions, comprising nearly one-third of all engineering students and roughly that percentage among working engineers. Because computers and electronics—both the product of electrical engineering technology—represent the totality of high technology to many people, this profession offers the most direct entry into high tech fields.

THE ROOTS OF ELECTRICAL ENGINEERING

Even though it is the largest engineering discipline, electrical engineering is also one of the youngest. There was hardly any electrical technology to speak of before the 1880s, when Thomas Edison's inventions were commercialized. But since then—what changes! Electrical illumination was shortly followed by electrical power (in the form of motors), telecommunications (in the form of the telephone and telegraph), entertainment (motion pictures and recordings) and, at the beginning of this century, radio.

In the 1920s, the first television cameras and receivers were invented, but it would be another twenty years before they became commercially available. By this time, so-called radio engineering was a strong profession of its own. It was out of radio technology that most electronic devices were invented. The development of the transistor in the early 1950s spurred the electronics industry forward, and by that time there were more radio engineers than electrical engineers, even though both were working on electrical technology. The Institute of Electrical Engineers (who represented primarily those involved with electricity generation and with the use of electricity for motors and heavy machinery) merged with the Institute of Radio Engineers in 1963, and the two professions have been identical ever since.

WHAT ELECTRICAL ENGINEERS DO

Even though we are in the midst of rapid technological change wrought by computers and electronics, most observers of the high tech scene expect even bigger and better advancements in the near future. The power of a computer that occupied an entire room just a generation ago now fits in the palm of one's hand, and it is realistically expected that the supercomputers of today, which can process billions of instructions per second, will be a common desktop tool in just a few years. One of the troublesome communications issues of today—how to fit television, radio, telephony, and data communications over a telecommunications wire so that all can be carried simultaneously—may be solved in the near future by advances in fiber optics.

The driving force for much of this innovation is the still-incredible shrinking power of the semiconductor chip. Fifty years ago, the technical capability of switching an electrical signal from *on* to *off* required a glass tube almost as big as a coffee cup. Twenty-five years ago, it required a transistor device about as big as a penny. Ten years ago, 64,000 transistors could be fitted in the space that a single transistor had occupied, and today, 16,000,000 of them can fit in that space. With each jump in capacity, it becomes easier to put electronics into all sorts of machines and devices—even our own bodies—and to provide stored instructions so that some purpose can be achieved.

These instructions—computer programming—remain a part of electrical engineering, although the growth of the computer science and engineering field as a distinct profession and college discipline has caused some of that work to move away from electrical engineering. Today, it is customary for electrical engineers to be primarily concerned with electrical and electronic hardware—the chips, circuit boards, data storage, and communications devices. Computer scientists and engineers, meanwhile, hold primary responsibility for electronic software—the programs and instructions that the hardware carry out. There remain substantial areas of overlap, however.

Although it is now a smaller part of the electrical engineering profession, power generation, storage, and use remain an important part of electrical engineering work. Electrical utilities are examining new options in generating power from cleaner, less-polluting sources. Nuclear power may re-emerge as the most viable power-generation option when, and if, the problems of radioactive waste disposal are solved. The conservation of electricity, through the use of better materials, electronic controls, and more sensible consumption patterns, is an important issue for power engineers today and will remain so in the future. Solar power, wind, water, and other sources of electrical energy will continue to be developed as practical alternatives to large power stations.

WHAT ELECTRICAL ENGINEERING STUDENTS STUDY

Once the fundamental principles of electricity, magnetism, and light were worked out by physicists and other researchers in the mid-1800s, a world of opportunities opened up for electrical engineers. This pattern is reflected in the education of electrical engineers on college campuses. Introductory courses in physics and mathematics provide the basic tools for working with electricity. The design of electrical circuits, in which components such as resistors, capacitors, and switches are assembled, is the next step. Finally, electronic circuit design is taught, along with complementary subjects such as materials science, computer programming, and computer theory.

Because there is so much technology to master and advances occur so rapidly in the field, it is quite common for electrical engineers to go on to graduate school after obtaining their bachelor's degree. Most electrical engineers, whether with a basic or advanced degree, work in design—figuring out better arrangements of electrical and electronic components to produce commercial products. A strong trend throughout electrical design practice is the incorporation of electronic devices into circuits. Most electrical companies, and all electronics companies, spend heavily on R&D. Many of them support large laboratories where the fundamental properties of new materials can be studied.

Until recently, the needs of the military were a strong trend in electronic development, both for weaponry and for such technical issues as communications and guidance. Today, the budget of the U.S. Department of Defense is shrinking, and questions are being raised as to the value of better military electronics when the peaceful uses of the technology are so important. It is impossible to say what the distant future holds in terms of world peace. Until recently, the competition between the United States and the Soviet Union for better military equipment led to many advances in electronics, aviation, space technology, and related electrical engineering fields. In the future, if military tensions continue to dwindle between the world superpowers, this competition will decline (though it will never disappear). For the short term, though, it makes practical sense to turn one's career aspirations to peaceful uses of electronics, rather than military ones.

There were about 22,000 bachelor's degree electrical engineering graduates per year in the United States in the late 1980s. In Canada, there were about 1,700 per year. The immediate job outlook is clouded by the reduction in military spending, which affects not only the aerospace companies that make aircraft, missiles, and other weapons, but also the electronics companies that are suppliers to the aerospace ones.

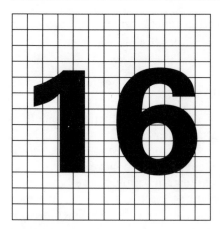

MECHANICAL ENGINEERING

Machines are a dominating element of modern life. From the microwave oven in the kitchen to the automobile in the garage to the power station down the road, machines affect every aspect of our daily lives. The mechanical engineering profession has played a major role in making this come about. Today's mechanical engineers are devising new types of robotics and automation techniques, space exploration vehicles, and pollution reduction technologies for power generation and waste disposal.

Mechanical engineering is the second-largest engineering discipline and as such is deeply involved in nearly every type of manufacturing activity and in service industries and government as well. Mechanical engineering has also taken very well to the advent of the computer: Much of the design work mechanical engineers perform is carried out on high-powered computers. Nor should it be overlooked that mechanical engineering is a critical technology for the design and manufacture of computers themselves.

THE ROOTS OF MECHANICAL ENGINEERING

While there were any number of machines and complex structures in ancient and medieval times, mechanical engineering really came into being during the Industrial Revolution in Europe in the first half of the nineteenth century. The development of steam power, which led to steam-powered locomotives and ships and provided a more dependable power source for factories than water wheels, was a key step.

During the latter half of the nineteenth century, mechanical engineering exploded in North America. The invention of the McCormack mechanical harvester, the repeating rifle, electrical generators, the telegraph, and the telephone were celebrated landmarks of new technology. Inventors like Alexander Graham Bell and Thomas Edison were national heros. At the end of that century, Henry Ford unveiled his gasoline-powered automobile, and the Wright brothers took their epochal flight at Kitty Hawk, North Carolina.

As significant as these new products were, it was equally important that mechanical engineering technology was instrumental in creating the new manufacturing methods that these devices required. The concept of the modern, mass-production factory, in which semiskilled workers repeated, very precisely, manufacturing steps in as little time as possible, allowed the new inventions to be marketed cheaply. Mass-production technology was so successful that by the 1920s, its proponents looked to it as a way of modeling all social behavior. The technocracy movement of that time was a strong effort to bring this about, but was met with disdain by the time the Depression rolled around.

The unifying aspect of most mechanical engineering technology is material objects in motion. Whether the object is a piston inside an automobile engine or the fluttering of an artificial heart valve inside a patient, materials and motion are the key.

In the era after World War II, as the automobile, the computer, and the jet airplane became common, everyday resources for society, mechanical engineering grew strong and prosperous. By the 1970s, though, it became clear that as successful as manufacturers had been in the United States, they were not keeping up with advances in Japan and Western Europe. New statistical measures of the quality of manufactured goods were called for, and this effort continues today.

WHAT MECHANICAL ENGINEERS DO

In the early 1980s, robotics was thought to be one of the highest of high technologies. Planners envisioned factories without a single worker, where robots would produce perfect products without human intervention. This vision has not come to pass, due primarily to the high cost of quality robotic equipment and the inability to program robots to resolve all the technical issues that a typical machine-tool worker has to deal with. Robotics is not dead—it is still a billion-dollar industry. But the initial vision of pervasive automation throughout all of manufacturing has faded to a more realistic view.

This view is quite thrilling all by itself. Manufacturers today have become extremely adept at applying microprocessors to all sorts of machinery. There are microchips under the hood of nearly all new cars, and fly-by-wire aircraft (which use computers to translate the guidance instructions of a pilot into the actual functions of controlling an aircraft) are now commercial.

This process will continue to intensify in coming years. Mechanical engineers are creating ever more sophisticated computer programs to monitor the quality of manufacturing processes and to run them safely and efficiently. These control networks are hooked into a supervisory level of computers, which automatically collect production data, analyze it, and make recommendations on how the process could be improved. At the management level, the data on plant operations are reviewed by yet another set of computers, and decisions are made by business managers on inventory levels, forecasted production, and production cost data. The use of statistical measures of production quantity and quality has increased dramatically.

WHAT MECHANICAL ENGINEERING STUDENTS STUDY

Mechanical engineering students take introductory courses in physics, chemistry, and mathematics. These are followed by the mechanical engineering curriculum, which includes such subjects as mechanics, thermodynamics, automation, and control. At the upper-level undergraduate and graduate levels, it is possible to concentrate in courses relating to a specific industry, such as aerospace, power generation, or transportation.

About 15,000 mechanical engineers graduated with bachelor's degrees annually during the late 1980s, according to federal data. In Canada, the figure has been around 1,700 each year. Enrollments have been declining slightly, and job prospects, while not especially bright, have been fairly steady.

PHYSICS

17

Physics is generally considered the king of sciences in that it addresses fundamental questions about matter, energy, and the universe. It is true that, armed with a doctorate degree in physics, one can address these issues, too. But most physics students stop after obtaining their bachelor's degree, and for these job candidates, careers in more applied fields open up. The most popular fields for physics employment are in electronics, materials science, and medical or scientific instrumentation. Until recently, there were many opportunities for doing defense-related work as well, but these opportunities are expected to decline in the near future.

THE ROOTS OF PHYSICS

There is a continuous history of physics from ancient times to today, especially if one includes astronomy (which is taught in conjunction with physics at many universities). In fact, the history of science is very often summed up as the history of physics, at least until this century. Famous names such as Aristotle, Ptolemy, Isaac Newton, and Albert Einstein are known to every science student.

In ancient times, physics was very much a part of philosophy and even religion; people tried to address human curiosity about the universe around them through whatever scientific means were at hand. By the Renaissance, however, physics had taken on a more earthly nature. Realizing that the Earth was not in the center of the solar system, or the universe itself, helped navigators formulate better methods of mapping the sky and of charting the transit of ships across oceans. By the Industrial Revolution of the 1800s, the knowledge that Isaac Newton had revealed about matter and energy helped researchers of that time devise better machines. Physics was also instrumental in developing the electromagnetic theory that inventors like Thomas Edison applied to create practical electrical machines.

At the close of the nineteenth century, the questions about the atomic nature of matter had led to the discovery of radioactivity and started the march toward the atomic bomb and nuclear energy. This greater understanding of the atom has influenced chemistry, medicine, and materials science, which are dominant themes in high technology today.

WHAT PHYSICISTS DO

Today, physics research marches on, as popular as ever, even though it very often deals with seemingly distant topics like the beginning of the universe or the nature of sub-subatomic matter that exists for only a minute fraction of a second before it disintegrates. While there are physicists who work strictly in such noncommercial areas as astronomy and subatomic matter, and there are others who work on commercial applications of electronics or materials, very often the two cross over. A development in the commercial arena, such as warm superconductors, leads to new fundamental knowledge about matter. Or a development in astrophysics, such as the nature of the fusion cycle that powers stars, leads to new knowledge in atomic energy.

The big distinction, then, among physicists is not whether the research is commercial or noncommercial (no one can predict which way such research will go), but rather between doctoral-level research and the R&D work that physics majors with only a bachelor's degree will do.

Such baccalaureate physicists fit very nicely into the electronics industry, where highly sophisticated instruments are used to manufacture semiconductor chips and other devices. Sometimes these graduates get involved in R&D, and sometimes they are strictly technical workers responsible for production of commercial products.

Another strong field for the physics undergraduate is in instrumentation. An instrument is simply some tool that helps measure physical properties. It can be as simple as a thermometer or as complex as a particle accelerator that generates high-level radiation. The growth of new materials science knowledge has enabled the production of all sorts of new instruments, including ones that measure atmospheric properties, provide chemical analysis of small amounts of matter, or detect extremely small amounts of valuable biochemicals during biotechnology research.

WHAT PHYSICS STUDENTS STUDY

Physics majors at college take plenty of math courses, including math courses that are taught in the physics department itself. These are followed by courses in atomic theory, astrophysics, and materials science. Solid-state physics is the term that usually describes courses relating to materials science and electronics, and employers will look for such courses in the school record of students they seek to hire into the electronics industry.

There were about 4,000 bachelor degrees in physics awarded each year in the late 1980s in the United States. About a quarter of these graduates traditionally go on to obtain graduate degrees.

Part Four
Choosing a
High Tech Career

EDUCATIONAL AND CAREER PLANNING

The information in this book is simply an introduction to high technology and the careers within that field. In practically each topic or academic discipline listed, there is easily enough further information to consider that would fill another book of this size.

LEARNING ABOUT HIGH TECH CAREERS

What should you do to get the information and make the best career choices? A good first step is to write to the professional organizations listed in the following pages. Most of them have career guidance packages that will provide more details about what is going on within these professions. Every professional society is eager to get more members because the number of members in an organization is a measure of its importance and power. So expect good treatment: a quick response to your letter and a hospitable reception when you address questions to them.

A second step is to follow your contact at the national level with contact at the local level. If you live near practically any major urban area—and quite a few suburban or rural areas as well—these professional societies will have local chapters that are accessible to you. Get in touch with the local leaders of these organizations and ask if you can attend the regular meetings, which are sometimes held on a monthly basis. Periodically, too, the local chapter will host a national meeting, which will bring professionals from around the country to your region. At the best organizations, the national meeting is usually an occasion for papers to be presented by experts in their field. These presentations are often very informative. Try to get permission to sit in on them.

In a similar vein, nearly every professional organization of any significant size has an in-house journal or magazine that informs its members of significant happenings within the profession. Usually, these journals are obtained through membership in the organization, which would keep most high-school students out of the picture.

Again, if you live in a major urban area, you can gain access to these journals by going to nearly any large urban library. If there is a college or university in your area, you will also find most of these journals at the school's library. (You will almost never find these publications for sale at a news stand, but that doesn't mean that they aren't worth reading.) Read the journals closely, especially those that report news of the profession as well as publish research papers. Look at the advertisements in them, and try to figure out of what value that equipment or service is to a profession.

It is worthwhile to read these journals or to attend these meetings not to gain useful technical knowledge that you can apply while you go on to college (although that is certainly possible), but to gain a sense of the people and issues within that profession. Leave yourself open to the "feel" of the information you are getting, rather than the factual content. Would you be happy with these people as your coworkers? Are the subjects that concern them something you are curious about?

There are, of course, many other official avenues for obtaining information about a high tech profession, often through your high-school science teachers or guidance counselors. Make use of them, too.

The value of all these forms of contact is to give you an insight into what the future holds and to provide role models of people whose work or attitudes toward their careers will help motivate you. Studying science or engineering at nearly any college is a difficult undertaking, and the programs are often too concentrated on technical learning and not concentrated enough on what to do with that technical learning. This is an unfortunate, but probably necessary, obstacle to a high tech career. Most science and engineering students are of little value to a researcher or employer until the basic technical knowledge is obtained.

MAKING YOUR CAREER CHOICES

Time after time, guidance counselors and career advisers when asked by a student, "What should I study, and what career should I follow?" tell the student: Do what you are good at and enjoy doing and what meets your needs for financial security. At the beginning of most people's careers, financial needs are not as great as they are later in life, so really the issue boils down to finding a field of education and work that interests you.

Frequently, however, too many students make decisions for a college major and a career on the basis of what is hot or in demand at the time they enter college. This is a serious mistake for several reasons.

First, it is often the case that what was a hot field when you entered college has cooled noticeably by the time you graduate. (Don't be totally alarmed if this is in fact what happens; there are things you can do to make the best of the situation.)

Second, you may be denying your true abilities if you study a subject only because of its assumed job potential after you graduate. Our daily work occupies at least half of our waking existence; why spend this time doing something that you do not enjoy? Moreover, the best work is usually performed by people who enjoy what they are doing. Do yourself and your future employer a favor and choose a major that fulfills your personal interests.

Third, it is becoming more and more uncommon for someone to study a professional topic in college, join a company to practice that profession, and spend the next forty years working at that job for one employer. More and more, people switch jobs, voluntarily or involuntarily, during their careers. Numerous surveys show that a worker who has had three or four employers by the time he or she is middle-aged earns more and has a higher position than one who does not move about. If you study a field that doesn't appeal to you to begin with, your ability to grow in that field or to use your job experience as a springboard to another line of work is limited.

Fourth, college is easy for many people, but it is not easy for many students who choose majors in science or engineering disciplines. The work is demanding, and the competition is often intense. It doesn't make sense to put yourself through a major that you have no personal attachment to.

College is a time to experiment, to find yourself in the various subjects and disciplines that you are exposed to. This experimenting works best when you give each subject your best shot. If you are majoring in something that is of no interest to you, you have limited your opportunities to experiment.

Having said all this, it may still be very difficult to select a major that you will enjoy. It is easy after college is done to look back at good and bad choices. It is very difficult to do this while looking ahead. This is where the familiarity with people who actually practice in a field that is of interest to you comes in. Ask them what they majored in and why. Ask them what was good and bad about their education, and how valuable it is to their work today. Take advantage of the experiences of others.

BACHELOR'S, MASTER'S, OR DOCTORATE?

In a great many professions, a bachelor's degree is sufficient. A student may *choose* to go on to graduate school, but except in selected areas like medicine or teaching, an advanced degree simply makes one somewhat more employable or possibly worth a higher salary. (In medicine and teaching, there are many career positions that simply are not accessible to the bachelor's graduate.)

In most of the sciences, there are two distinct tracks that graduates can follow based on their degree level. In most cases, R&D positions are open to those with advanced degrees, but relatively limited for those with only a bachelor's degree. If you want to work in the laboratories of major corporations, top universities, or prestigious private research organizations, make preparations for continuing your schooling. You might need to alter your undergraduate course load somewhat to take courses that will be a useful preparation to graduate school (acquiring expertise in a foreign language is one example).

This certainly doesn't mean that only a Ph.D. scientist can be a high tech worker. The work in commercializing new scientific knowledge in the form of useful products requires extensive work in process design, manufacturing methods, marketing, and technical service. All these job positions are usually available to the bachelor's graduate.

While it is possible to obtain a master's degree in most of the sciences, there are not many job positions specifically geared to the master's-level graduate. Having this degree certainly makes the graduate more employable, relative to those with only a bachelor's degree, but very often, the master's graduate winds up competing against bachelor's-degree holders for the same jobs. Most teaching positions at universities require the doctorate; most R&D positions in laboratories call for that degree as well.

In the engineering disciplines, there are five distinct educational goals that can be sought. One is the bachelor's degree alone, which is the training that most engineers stop with. It is a testament to the value of an engineering degree that very often this is all the college-level education that an engineer needs for a lifelong career. To be sure, a good engineer will continue to learn as his or her career progresses, by attending technical meetings, signing up for seminars sponsored by an employer, or gaining admission to company training programs. Many of the professional societies listed in this section sponsor continuing education programs to further enhance engineers' skills.

Many baccalaureate engineers go on to obtain a master's in business administration (MBA) with the expectation that the two degrees will help them rise into management positions in technology-driven companies. Some engineers feel that the conventional MBA degree, which usually involves the study of finance, economics, and related topics, is not closely enough connected to technology management. For this reason, some schools have started programs in management of technology or manufacturing technology as a better alternative to the conventional MBA.

Another choice is to pursue a professional engineer's (P.E.) license. This certification is provided by all fifty states and requires passing two tests and gaining several years' experience in working under the guidance of engineers who themselves have P.E. licenses. With a P.E. license, an engineer has a more prestigious achievement record to present to potential employers and can also do certain types of work (the design of public buildings, for example) that unlicensed engineers are not permitted to do.

There are definitely good reasons for having a P.E. license; nevertheless, only about a quarter or so of working engineers have bothered to earn it, and most of those are civil engineers. The simple fact of the matter is that in many types of work, a P.E. license is not a requirement.

The fourth choice is to obtain a master's degree in engineering. Most of the time, this degree level demonstrates to an employer that a job candidate has a serious commitment to the technology of the candidate's major. In certain fields, such as semiconductor design, computer science, factory automation, and others, the technology is moving so fast and the necessary knowledge for professional practice is growing so large that a master's degree is simply a way of keeping up with change. For this reason, many engineers get a job after earning their bachelor's degree and then study for a master's at evening school. Often, an engineer's employer will cover the cost of this advanced education.

A variation on the master's-degree track is to obtain a master's in an engineering or science program other than what one studied as an undergraduate. This doesn't work equally well for all combinations of undergraduate and master's programs. Depending on the choices, the student may wind up needing more undergraduate-level courses to meet the requirements of the master's program or may find that the master's degree in one field has little to do with employment in another. This is definitely a situation where career advice from college deans or from employment professionals is a help.

The fifth option, of course, is to obtain a doctorate degree in engineering. This qualifies the engineer to teach and to perform R&D in nearly all technologies. There are Ph.D. engineers who perform basic research, developing new techniques for microelectronics design, writing computer software, or designing advanced materials. There are others whose work is geared more toward applications in the commercial world, such as designing better automobiles, more energy-efficient power generators, or more wholesome foods. The choice is up to the individual.

As all these choices indicate, there are many career paths open to the high tech worker. The educational requirements are demanding, but the rewards are plentiful. Contact the following professional and educational organizations for more information. Make researching a career as important as the study you put into any of the courses you are taking now or while you are in college.

PROFESSIONAL AND EDUCATIONAL ORGANIZATIONS

Alliance for Engineering in
  Medicine and Biology
1101 Connecticut Ave., NW
Washington, DC 20036

American Academy of
  Environmental Engineers
132 Holiday Court
Suite 206
Annapolis, MD 21401

American Association for the
Advancement of Science
1333 H St., NW
Washington, DC 20005

American Chemical Society
1155 16th St., NW
Washington, DC 20036

American Entomological Society
1900 Race St.
Philadelphia, PA 19103

American Forestry Society
P.O. Box 2000
Washington, DC 20013

American Industrial Hygiene
Association
475 Wolf Ledges Parkway
Akron, OH 44311

American Institute of
Aeronautics and Astronautics
370 L'Enfant Promenade, SW
Washington, DC 20024

American Institute of Chemical
Engineers
345 East 47th St.
New York, NY 10017

American Institute of Mining,
Metallurgical and Petroleum
Engineers (AIME)
345 East 47th St.
New York, NY 10017

American Institute of Physics
335 East 45th St.
New York, NY 10017

American Institute of Plant
Engineers
3975 Erie Ave.
Cincinnati, OH 45208

American Mathematical Society
201 Charles St.
Providence, RI 02904

American Meteorological Society
45 Beacon St.
Boston, MA 02108

American Nuclear Society
555 North Kensington Ave.
La Grange Park, IL 60525

American Physical Society
(Physics) (APS)
335 E. 45th St.
New York, NY 10017

American Public Health
Association
1015 15th St., NW
Washington, DC 20005

American Society of Agricultural
Engineers
2950 Niles Rd.
St. Joseph, MI 49085

American Society of Agronomy
677 South Segoe Rd.
Madison, WI 53711

American Society of Civil
Engineers
Student Services Dept.
345 East 47th St.
New York, NY 10017

American Society of Heating,
Refrigerating and
Air-Conditioning Engineers,
Inc. (ASHRAE)
1791 Tulie Circle, NE
Atlanta, GA 30329

American Society of Mechanical
Engineers
345 East 47th St.
New York, NY 10017

American Society for
Microbiology
1913 Eye St., NW
Washington, DC 20006

American Society of Naval
Engineers
1452 Duke St.
Alexandria, VA 22314

American Society of Safety
Engineers
1800 E. Oakton St.
Des Plaines, IL 60018

ASM International (American
Society for Metals)
Metals Park, OH 44073

Canadian Aeronautics and Space
Institute
Suite 601
222 Somerset St. W
Ottawa, Ontario
Canada K2P 0J1

Canadian Council of Professional
Engineers
116 Albert St.
Suite 401
Ottawa, Ontario
Canada K1P 5G3

Canadian Forestry Association
185 Somerset St. W
Ottawa, Ontario
Canada K2P 0J2

Canadian Geotechnical Society
170 Attwell Drive
Suite 602
Rexdale, Ontario
Canada M9W 5Z5

Canadian Society for Chemical
Engineering
1785 Alta Vista Drive
Ottawa, Ontario
Canada K1G 3Y6

Canadian Society for Civil
Engineering
700 EIC Bldg.
2050 Mansfield St.
Montreal, Quebec
Canada H3A 1Z2

Canadian Society for Electrical
Engineering
700 EIC Bldg.
2050 Mansfield St.
Montreal, Quebec
Canada H3A 1Z2

Canadian Society for Mechanical
Engineering
700 EIC Bldg.
2050 Mansfield St.
Montreal, Quebec
Canada H3A 1Z2

Data Processing Management
Association
505 Busse Highway
Park Ridge, IL 60068

Engineering Institute of Canada
700 EIC Bldg.
2050 Mansfield St.
Montreal, Quebec
Canada H3A 1Z2

Geological Society of America
3300 Penrose Place
Boulder, CO 80301

Institute of Electrical and
Electronics Engineers, Inc.
345 East 47th St.
New York, NY 10017

Institute of Industrial Engineers
25 Technology Park
Norcross, GA 30092

Instrument Society of America
Education Services
67 Alexander Drive
P.O. Box 12277
Research Triangle Park, NC
27709

Junior Engineering Technical
Society (JETS)
1420 King St.
Alexandria, VA 22314

Marine Technology Society
2000 Florida Ave., NW
Suite 500
Washington, DC 20009

The Metallurgical Society
420 Commonwealth Drive
Warrendale, PA 15086

National Action Council for
   Minorities in Engineering
3 West 35th St.
New York, NY 10001

National Institute of Ceramic
   Engineers
65 Ceramic Drive
Columbus, OH 43214

National Society of Professional
   Engineers (NSPE)
1420 King St.
Alexandria, VA 22314

Operations Research Society of
   America
Mt. Royal & Guilford Ave.
Baltimore, MD 21202

Optical Society of America
1816 Jefferson Place, NW
Washington, DC 20036

Society for the Advancement of
   Material & Process Engineering
843 W. Glentana St. (Box 2459)
Covina, CA 91722

Society of Automotive Engineers
400 Commonwealth Drive
Warrendale, PA 15096

Society of Fire Protection
   Engineers
60 Batterymarch St.
Boston, MA 02110

Society of Manufacturing
   Engineers
One SME Drive
Dearborn, MI 48121

Society of Naval Architects and
   Marine Engineers
One World Trade Center, Suite
   1369
New York, NY 10048

Society of Plastics Engineers
14 Fairfield Drive
Brookfield, CT 06804

Society of Women Engineers
345 East 47th St.
New York, NY 10017

VGM CAREER BOOKS

OPPORTUNITIES IN
*Available in both paperback and
hardbound editions*
Accounting
Acting
Advertising
Aerospace
Agriculture
Airline
Animal and Pet Care
Architecture
Automotive Service
Banking
Beauty Culture
Biological Sciences
Biotechnology
Book Publishing
Broadcasting
Building Construction Trades
Business Communication
Business Management
Cable Television
Carpentry
Chemical Engineering
Chemistry
Child Care
Chiropractic Health Care
Civil Engineering
Cleaning Service
Commercial Art and Graphic Design
Computer Aided Design and
    Computer Aided Mfg.
Computer Maintenance
Computer Science
Counseling & Development
Crafts
Culinary
Customer Service
Dance
Data Processing
Dental Care
Direct Marketing
Drafting
Electrical Trades
Electronic and Electrical Engineering
Electronics
Energy
Engineering
Engineering Technology
Environmental
Eye Care
Fashion
Fast Food
Federal Government
Film
Financial
Fire Protection Services
Fitness
Food Services
Foreign Language
Forestry
Gerontology
Government Service
Graphic Communications
Health and Medical
High Tech
Home Economics
Hospital Administration
Hotel & Motel Management
Human Resources Management
    Careers
Information Systems
Insurance
Interior Design
International Business
Journalism
Laser Technology
Law

Law Enforcement and Criminal Justice
Library and Information Science
Machine Trades
Magazine Publishing
Management
Marine & Maritime
Marketing
Materials Science
Mechanical Engineering
Medical Technology
Metalworking
Microelectronics
Military
Modeling
Music
Newspaper Publishing
Nursing
Nutrition
Occupational Therapy
Office Occupations
Opticianry
Optometry
Packaging Science
Paralegal Careers
Paramedical Careers
Part-time & Summer Jobs
Performing Arts
Petroleum
Pharmacy
Photography
Physical Therapy
Physician
Plastics
Plumbing & Pipe Fitting
Podiatric Medicine
Postal Service
Printing
Property Management
Psychiatry
Psychology
Public Health
Public Relations
Purchasing
Real Estate
Recreation and Leisure
Refrigeration and Air Conditioning
Religious Service
Restaurant
Retailing
Robotics
Sales
Sales & Marketing
Secretarial
Securities
Social Science
Social Work
Speech-Language Pathology
Sports & Athletics
Sports Medicine
State and Local Government
Teaching
Technical Communications
Telecommunications
Television and Video
Theatrical Design & Production
Transportation
Travel
Trucking
Veterinary Medicine
Visual Arts
Vocational and Technical
Warehousing
Waste Management
Welding
Word Processing
Writing
Your Own Service Business

CAREERS IN Accounting; Advertising;
Business; Communications; Computers;
Education; Engineering; Health Care;
High Tech; Law; Marketing; Medicine;
Science

CAREER DIRECTORIES
Careers Encyclopedia
Dictionary of Occupational Titles
Occupational Outlook Handbook

CAREER PLANNING
Admissions Guide to Selective
    Business Schools
Career Planning and Development for
    College Students and Recent
    Graduates
Careers Checklists
Careers for Animal Lovers
Careers for Bookworms
Careers for Culture Lovers
Careers for Foreign Language
    Aficionados
Careers for Good Samaritans
Careers for Gourmets
Careers for Nature Lovers
Careers for Numbers Crunchers
Careers for Sports Nuts
Careers for Travel Buffs
Guide to Basic Resume Writing
Handbook of Business and
    Management Careers
Handbook of Health Care Careers
Handbook of Scientific and
    Technical Careers
How to Change Your Career
How to Choose the Right Career
How to Get and Keep
    Your First Job
How to Get into the Right Law School
How to Get People to Do Things
    Your Way
How to Have a Winning Job Interview
How to Land a Better Job
How to Make the Right Career Moves
How to Market Your College Degree
How to Prepare a *Curriculum Vitae*
How to Prepare for College
How to Run Your Own Home Business
How to Succeed in Collge
How to Succeed in High School
How to Write a Winning Resume
Joyce Lain Kennedy's Career Book
Planning Your Career of Tomorrow
Planning Your College Education
Planning Your Military Career
Planning Your Young Child's
    Education
Resumes for Advertising Careers
Resumes for College Students & Recent
    Graduates
Resumes for Communications Careers
Resumes for Education Careers
Resumes for High School Graduates
Resumes for High Tech Careers
Resumes for Sales and Marketing Careers
Successful Interviewing for College
    Seniors

SURVIVAL GUIDES
Dropping Out or Hanging In
High School Survival Guide
College Survival Guide

VGM Career Horizons
a division of *NTC Publishing Group*
4255 West Touhy Avenue
Lincolnwood, Illinois 60646-1975